# ETHICS AND THE EMPLOYEE-CENTRIC FIRM

## JOHN E. WALKER

Two Harbors Press
Minneapolis, MN

Copyright © 2011 by John E. Walker.

**TWOHARBORS**
WWW.TWOHARBORSPRESS.COM

Two Harbors Press
212 3rd Avenue North, Suite 290
Minneapolis, MN 55401
612.455.2293
www.TwoHarborsPress.com

All rights reserved. No part of this publication may be reproduced, stored in a retrieval system, or transmitted, in any form or by any means, electronic, mechanical, photocopying, recording, or otherwise, without the prior written permission of the author.

ISBN-13: 978-1-937293-56-7
LCCN: 2011940243

Distributed by Itasca Books

Cover Design and Typeset by Sophie Chi

*Printed in the United States of America*

# Dedication

It gives me great pleasure to dedicate this book to:
John E. Walker, Sr.,
Professor Hugh H. Macaulay,
and the employees of Andesa Services
past, present, and future.

# Table of Contents

*Acknowledgments*..................................................*ix*

*Introduction*......................................................*xi*

## Chapter One:....................................1
My Father's Compass

## Chapter Two:..................................17
The End Justifies the Means—Or Does It?

## Chapter Three:...............................25
The Shepherd's Way

## Chapter Four:.................................35
The Nature of the Firm

## Chapter Five:..................................43
Application of Ethics to the Firm

## Chapter Six:...................................51
The Birth of Andesa

## Chapter Seven: ..................................71
Formalizing the Culture, 1983–2002

## Chapter Eight: ..................................89
Trial by Fire, 2003–2011

## Chapter Nine: ..................................99
Concluding Remarks

## Appendix A: ......................................107
Andesa Timeline

## Appendix B: ......................................109
The Evolution of Andesa's Management Team

## Acknowledgments

Several years ago, the employees of Andesa Services, Inc., a firm I helped to establish in 1983, asked that I document the founding of the company. Immediately, I thought it was a good idea, but I also wondered why. So I asked them. I am pleased that their primary motivation was a desire to have the firm's existing culture preserved. Further, they believed that memorializing the founding of Andesa would provide a template for future growth of both the firm and its individual employees.

Last year the Strom Thurmond Institute of Government and Public Affairs at Clemson University invited me to become a Senior Scholar with the institute. While discussing what I might do in this regard, I mentioned my passion for Andesa and its staff. After I described Andesa and its unique culture, the institute staff proposed that I write a book about the firm as an activity of the institute.

For my own part, I have, for some time, wanted to reach out to business people and share the story of Andesa with the hope that it will encourage managers to consider the crucial role environment plays in their firms. The more I talked about an ethical environment to people at Andesa and the Thurmond Institute, the more I came to believe that it was time to tell the story. I am thankful for their encouragement.

In the telling of this story, I am indebted to many, beyond those to whom this book is dedicated. The Strom Thurmond Institute staff has encouraged and supported me in many ways.

Dr. Robert Becker, Institute Director, and Dr. Clint Whitehurst, Institute Senior Scholar, were both critical to the undertaking of this project, and Dr. Whitehurst provided guidance and advice from beginning to end. Dr. Daniel Wueste, Director of the Robert J. Rutland Center for Ethics at Clemson University, was indispensable with his advice and editing. My long-term friend V. Barry Young provided comments and helpful editing on all aspects of the book. Clemson Professor Emeritus Bobby McCormick provided help (especially with Chapter Four) and general encouragement. Members of the Clemson Department of Economics and employees of Andesa provided various comments. I was fortunate to have the services of Emily Wood, an editor extraordinaire. She is a believer in the cause and was a soul mate in helping me tell my story. She was active beyond expectation, and I very much appreciate her assistance. And last, but not least, I thank my wife, Diane, for her forbearance through this project and for her graphics expertise.

Of course, all errors were incorporated without the need for assistance.

# Introduction

*I think of Andesa as a firm which has a soul. To say that a firm has a soul is to say that it has incorporated into its operating procedures strong ethical values and an uncompromising concern for the welfare of its employees. One of my greatest achievements is that I have been part of the creation of just such a firm*

– Andesa Services, Inc.

In the most basic terms, Andesa provides administrative services for niche market life insurance products to and on behalf of large life insurance companies. Andesa provides services in three major areas. First, we calculate, store, and retrieve life insurance policy values. Second, we provide the tools and data to allow our clients and their sales people to properly illustrate future values of life insurance policies. And third, we provide the tools and data to facilitate the management of these life insurance policies within the context of the plans for which they were acquired.

The life insurance policies that we administer are tailored to meet demanding requirements. Policy administration is more complex and the standards of performance are more demanding than those of standard life insurance policies. Accordingly, the nature of the business requires that we maintain a staff of highly qualified personnel to design, build, and operate custom systems on behalf of our clients. Most of these systems are automated computer systems operating with software written by Andesa staff.

Andesa is a good company; it serves its clients well. Customer satisfaction is surveyed annually, and we consistently rank well above the norm. But it is the manner in which we provide these services that defines Andesa. By approaching each and every task with the welfare of our employees in mind, Andesa has built an employee-centric environment, and it is this component of Andesa that entitles it to be called a firm with a soul.

When I think of soul, I think of passion to do something significant and admirable. I think of core values. At Andesa this means honesty, respect, integrity, responsibility, courage, and initiative. We believe that without the first four, any member of an organization will have a distorted view of his role. Without courage to back up one's view and initiative to follow through, the powerful qualities of honesty, respect, integrity, and responsibility will lie dormant. At Andesa, we incorporate these core values into a wholesome environment by adhering to a set of operational guidelines that acknowledge the value of our employees as well as our clients and owners. These operational guidelines are discussed in detail in the chapters chronicling the development of Andesa.

While the employee-centric approach adopted by Andesa is critical to the healthy existence of a firm, it is not limited to the firm. It is universally applicable to any organization of people who act with a common purpose. In fact, the most valuable application may well be to governmental, religious, or educational organizations. The business firm is the focal point of this book simply because it is where the bulk of my experience lies. In fact, it is where the bulk of most people's experience lies: What single activity consumes as much time with such great affect on both the worker and the worker's family as does his or her job? As such, the firm plays a critical role in our democratic form of society. It is true that the business firm provides goods and services to consumers, and, if operated inefficiently, it will not survive long within a free market society. But it also is true that, unless operated with a soul, a firm will fail to live up to its critical role of reinforcing good citizenship in its employees.

Andesa did not simply happen. It was developed with a great deal of thought over a long period of time. This book is the story of that journey, a journey that began with an ill-defined search for a healthy environment for employees of a business firm and led ultimately to the creation of Andesa. This is not a book about the idealistic formation of a perfect company. The reality is that human shortcomings posed many hurdles for Andesa along the way. Growth was at times difficult, and transitions were rough. A soul does not ensure an easy time of it; quite the opposite. But it does provide the firm with a moral compass and the wherewithal to weather almost any storm.

By all measures, Andesa is a successful company today. Employees like working for Andesa, clients are pleased with the services it provides, shareholders are well compensated for the financial resources they provide, and society is well served by its employee-centric approach. While many factors have contributed to this success, it is the unique vision of the company that is addressed in this book. Andesa's vision has been the cornerstone for its success; it is the foundation upon which Andesa has built its contributions to society.

*Chapter One*

# MY FATHER'S COMPASS

It would make little sense to begin the story of Andesa anywhere but at my father's side, because he was my role model, and hence, in a way, the role model for Andesa. John Walker, Sr. was a good man. He cared deeply about right and wrong and didn't believe in excuses when it came to unethical behavior. He took his responsibilities seriously, including that of being a father; and while my time with him was short, it was time well spent. His loving guidance helped make me the person I am today.

I was born the son of a career army officer. I was an army brat. In my youth, I resented the term, which my classmates used almost as a taunt. I knew it was more like a badge of honor among army personnel, but it made me feel different from my friends, and what kid wants to be different? While I have grown to appreciate and embrace my early connection to the United States Army, back then I didn't think much about a soldier's dedication or his contributions to society, including my father's. It wasn't until I was eighteen—a freshman in college and my father recently deceased—that I really began to contemplate who he was.

When my father was eighteen, his father was murdered for refusing to turn a blind eye on the bootlegging activities of a local bigwig. Prohibition was the law then, and he was a deputy sheriff, sworn to uphold it. This story alone suggests that he was the honorable sort of man my father came to be. My father's mother had died earlier from complications of giving birth, so with his father's death he and his two young sisters became orphans. I know little of this period other than that they were taken in by an aunt, they were poor, and life was hard. My father was fortunate enough to receive a scholarship to attend The Clemson Agricultural College of South Carolina (now known as Clemson University). He made the most of it, graduating with a BS in civil engineering. He apparently liked the military life he experienced at Clemson. Immediately after graduating as an honor military graduate, he entered the United States Army as a regular army second lieutenant and remained a soldier for the rest of his life.

The picture on the right is of my father early in his career as a US Army infantry lieutenant.

In 1936, the year I was born, my father was transferred from Portland, Maine, to Chilkoot Barracks, just outside the city of Haines, Alaska. An infantry captain at the time, he was given command of one of the post's two rifle companies. During his time at Chilkoot, my father displayed a natural talent for turning recruits into soldiers.

As a consequence of this experience, for the next six years he was transferred from one duty station to another to impart his methods. My mother kept a scrapbook of newspaper accounts of his innovative techniques and successful results. The scrapbook, together with most of our personal effects, was placed in storage in Kentucky while my father was overseas in the China-Burma-India Theater during WWII. In September 1946, when my father returned to the United States, he arranged for the stored possessions to be transported to our new home in Jacksonville. Somewhere between Kentucky and Florida, the moving van caught fire. The entire van and its contents burned to ashes.

We lived in many places before I was even old enough to start school. I don't remember where I went to kindergarten, only that I had to attend summer school because I could not read. When my father went to war, my mother relocated our family to St. Augustine to be close to extended family. I attended first, second, and third grades there before moving to Jacksonville when my father returned from overseas. My best guess is that I attended ten different schools in the United States, stretching along the east coast from Rhode Island to Florida, before we moved to Germany in 1950 where I began high school. We returned to the States in the middle of my junior year, and in 1954 I obtained my high school diploma from Washington-Lee High School in Arlington, Virginia.

I saw little of my father before and during WWII and not as much of him as I would have liked after his return from the war, but our constant moving ensured that I saw a great deal else. The geography, culture, and educational environment of my first eighteen years were ever-changing. The fact that I remember only three classmates' names is a measure of the difficulty of this lifestyle, but I am convinced that it helped to create in me an inquisitive mind, one open to the different customs, beliefs, and values I experienced in others. And perhaps it was this openness that allowed me to recognize and appreciate my father's values and the central role they played in his life.

In August of 1946, my father came home from the war. I was ten years old and set to begin a fourth year of school in St. Augustine. But my father had been assigned to the Jacksonville area administrative command, so we packed up and moved.

Our first home in Jacksonville was a quaint house on a large, overgrown lot. It was there, in the weedy backyard of a rental house, that I came to know my father. He had grown up on a farm in rural South Carolina, and I discovered that he still loved working the land. I believe he missed it. The day we arrived, he started clearing the yard and recruited me to be his helper. Amidst the bramble, we found a neglected arbor and a persimmon tree; the next day, a giant old pecan tree. While cutting grass that was nearly as tall as I with a sickle, we discovered a hidden gold fish pond, full of murky water and a school of the biggest goldfish I had ever seen. We taught ourselves how to harvest fruit and nuts from the trees, train vines on the arbor, and care for the fish. I remember this as a wonderful time of becoming reacquainted with my father.

The next year, we moved to another rental house in another section of town and began all over again. Then on to Rhode Island, where we tackled yet another yard. There my father taught me to bowl. He gave me his old army-issue hobnailed boots when a friend invited me to join him trapping muskrats and skunk. At the age of thirteen I was thrilled to find that my father's boots fit my feet. Working together on yards or projects or "hunting" expeditions became a theme between my father and me. Quickly we established a pattern of spending time together working at something we both enjoyed. It was a pattern we would follow until his death.

People say my father looked like John Wayne. He was six-foot one-inch, two hundred pounds, and in excellent shape.

The picture on the right is of my father taken in Burma or China during WWII as a US Army infantry lt. colonel.

He started a fitness regimen as a young man and never gave it up. Like John Wayne in any one of his westerns, my father was a man of few words, but those words meant a lot, and you would do well to heed them. That's not to say he was rough; he wasn't. Or loud; he wasn't. He had a quiet confidence about him that spoke louder and more persuasively than any belligerence would have. He had seriousness written all over him, from head to foot, and if you didn't look carefully, you would surely miss his flashes of mischief. Most obvious in my father's countenance was the sobriety with which he lived by his values. Even as a child, I could see it.

One of my earliest lessons in the nuances of my father's convictions occurred in 1950, the year I turned fourteen. We were living in Sheffield, Alabama, awaiting transfer to Germany. My mother had been raised in Sheffield, and she, my sister, and I frequently lived there for short periods while my father completed housing arrangements at his new duty stations. This time, he was with us. He and my mother and I were playing three-handed bridge when mother, frustrated by a night of unlucky hands, blurted out in anger, "I wouldn't be losing every hand if you both weren't cheating!"

"I am not cheating," I said to my mother, in a voice as calm as I could muster. "And I won't play bridge with anyone who says I am." Then I stood and stormed out of the room. My father was hard on my heels. I imagined him being as affronted as I at having been accused of cheating. I saw his exit as solidarity in protest of my mother's accusation.

But when my father caught up with me in the next room, he sat me down. He pulled up a chair and sat facing me, knee to knee. Then he looked me straight in the eye. "In this family, we do not treat our mothers with disrespect," he told me in a low voice. Then he explained, calmly but firmly, that although my mother was not herself, that did not give me liberty to be rude to her. I was shattered by the disappointment I saw in his eyes, and my vision began to spin. I all but fainted. This is the first and only memory I have of facing my father after failing to measure up to the values he held so dear.

Nineteen fifty-one was a time of changing national security, the early days of the cold war. It was also a time when my father's duties allowed him to spend a bit more time with me. We had just moved into requisitioned housing in Kesselstadt, Germany, a charming village about ten miles west of Hanau where my father, a colonel now, was the commanding officer of the Hanau sub-post. Our house, a three-story mansion with eight bedrooms, was one in a group of four houses that had been requisitioned from the wealthy citizens of Kesselstadt. A doctor and his family had lived in it prior to our moving in. The other houses were occupied by two brigadier generals and an American representative of the high commissioners of occupied Germany. The fifth house in the neighborhood belonged to the mayor of Kesselstadt. I was enrolled in an American high school about twenty miles away in Frankfurt, but I spent much of my free time with my friends on the base in Hanau. Most of the American military personnel lived on base, and a military bus transported their children to and from the school in Frankfurt each day. Frequently, I would take the bus to the base after school instead of going home, and I would walk to my father's office at the end of the day to catch a ride home with him.

One day I was sitting in the reception area outside his office, waiting for him to finish his work, when I heard him coldly exclaim, "I'll be damned if I'll do that!" I don't believe I had ever heard him raise his voice. I think he was embarrassed that I had heard the outburst, because on the way home a little while later, he explained that he was being pressured to approve a specific location for the construction of badly-needed housing for additional troops relocating to his sub-post. "Son," he said to me, "there are people who want to build this housing in an area that I am convinced will poorly influence our soldiers. It's an area that will contribute to the deterioration of their moral well-being, and I simply will not tolerate that." He was resolute. Even though the pressure was coming from higher ranking officers, he stood his ground.

This event seemed to start something between my father and me. It triggered several other discussions about values. While he was harsh in his assessment of the German officers who cooperated with what came to be known as the Holocaust, he openly admired the professionalism, honesty, and integrity of the German officer corps. "If you tell a man the truth," he said any time he mentioned honesty, "you need not worry about remembering what you told him." He had many sayings like that. My favorite was, "Fool me once, shame on you. Fool me twice, shame on me." I learned that my father put the emphasis on the first part. He believed strongly in trusting one's fellow man until actions proved the trust to be misplaced. To not trust someone was to strip him of his dignity, and my father was adamant about preserving dignity.

I remember another time waiting for my father outside his office in Hanau. A young corporal came into the reception area and sat down in the chair next to me. "Are you Colonel

Walker's son?" he asked. I told him I was, and he told me he thought my father was a fine man.

"Are you waiting to see him?" I asked.

"Yes," he said. "I'm in trouble." He looked a lot like I imagine I looked after disappointing my father.

I didn't ask, but he went on to tell me that, early on, back when he was a private, he had done something exceptional. He had shown initiative, and my father noticed. "He brought me in and promoted me to corporal, just like that." But then, the corporal told me, he had screwed up. "Your dad is gonna take this stripe away from me," he said.

He wasn't in my father's office for long. When he came out, he nodded at me, and he said, "Yeah, I lost the stripe." It was obvious that he was disappointed, but it was also clear that he knew he deserved the demotion. My father was not vindictive, but he was unmistakably and unequivocally judicial.

My father led by example. His commitment to duty knew few bounds, and in this he was ever-vigilant. One day, while he was dressed in civilian clothes, he drove up to the post gate with my mother and me in our personal car. The car was a black 1946 Pontiac with American license plates, and the sentry waved us through. My father stopped the car twenty feet or so inside the gate, rolled down the window, and motioned for the sentry to approach. "Do you know who I am?" he asked the guard. The guard did not. "Why, then," my father asked, "have you admitted me without requiring me to show positive identification?" The guard stammered some excuse that clearly did not impress my father, and for every inadequate answer the guard provided, my father had an additional question. I felt the sentry's increasing discomfort and found myself growing uneasy as well. At long last, the sentry got it right. "Sir," he finally said, "may I see your identification?" After examining my father's military ID, he saluted my father and stepped back.

As soon as we pulled away, I asked, "Why'd you do that, Dad?"

"We could have been Soviet agents for all he knew," he replied. "I won't condone sloppy security."

One of the last serious discussions I remember having with him was about Senator Joseph McCarthy. He despised the man and his tactics. As a result, I was fascinated when McCarthy became a daily news item. I may well have been the only senior at Washington-Lee High School who raced home to watch the Army-McCarthy hearings on television. It took very little time before I shared my father's disdain for the senator.

Holding to his principles was not something my father did gracefully. He did not have the gift of opposing another person's will in a way that would make the person thank him for his counsel. He was a plain-spoken, country boy who said his piece. He was never mean, but he was frank. I asked him once—I think it was soon after the incident with the sentry—if he would be promoted to general soon. He grinned and said, "I will never be a general. I've stepped on too many toes in my career." His admission surprised me. Other than the housing disagreement, he had never discussed his work difficulties with me. Shortly after his death, my mother explained that in spite of his stoicism, his military time in Germany had been stressful and draining. Only when I was in Germany as a first lieutenant did I learn what had transpired during the time our family lived there. The US armed forces were being heavily re-arranged to better resist any invasion into West Germany by Soviet forces. The Fulda gap was one of three routes Soviet armor could use to invade West Germany, and it was located within the boundaries of my father's sub-post.

My father's blunt refusal to compromise principles meant that he had many detractors, but he had his share of supporters as well. One of them was the commanding general of a Seventh

Army Corps stationed in and around his sub-post in Hanau. My father had served under him years earlier and earned the general's respect. In the midst of the housing conflict, the general and his wife called upon my parents one evening for dinner and conversation. I was not invited to join them, but my mother told me about it afterward. The general wanted the opportunity to convey to my father, in an unofficial capacity, that he fully supported my father's position. For an officer three grades higher to make this effort was remarkable.

My father had a demanding schedule of duty while we were in Germany, but he managed to find time for family. One weekend in 1950 we piled into the Pontiac and drove to Oberammergau to watch a performance of the Passion Play. Hitler had suspended performances of the play in the early 1930s, and it had just returned to the Oberammergau Passion Playhouse that spring. On another occasion, we spent a week in the Garmisch-Partenkirchen area on holiday. During a trip to Holland we stayed at a very exclusive inn, the first such luxury I had ever experienced. Honestly, our taste of high-class living was only made possible by the depressed level of European economies at that time. This was not the way we typically traveled. One evening at dinner, the wine steward approached the table and presented my father with a wine list. Caring little for wine and knowing even less about it, he joked, "Let my wife select, it's her birthday." We thought nothing more about it until the end of the meal when the string quartet stuck up the refrain of "Happy Birthday" and our waiter brought an impressive lighted cake to our table.

My father always showed an interest in my high school activities, but he was especially supportive when I took up target shooting. I was fourteen, and my Christmas present that year was a Stevens over & under .22-cal rifle/ .410 shotgun. We started spending a lot of time shooting at indoor and outdoor ranges. Satisfied that I had learned proper safety procedures and was comfortable with guns, the next Christmas my parents gave me a Remington 12-gauge automatic shotgun. My father bought himself a double barrel 12-gauge shotgun, and we began shooting clay pigeons together in earnest. He had not fired a shotgun in decades, but together we had a great time target shooting and both became quite proficient. He had always treated me with respect, but even at the age of fifteen I recognized this as something new; it was adult respect.

While we were still in Germany, he took me to a gun club where they made custom rifles. "This is a beauty," I said, holding a sleek hunting rifle. "I'll tell you what, son," he said to me after looking it over. "Save your money. I'll match you dollar for dollar." He didn't tell me that he had confidence that I could handle a powerful weapon. He didn't explain that he was challenging me to work hard for something I wanted. That wasn't his style. He just made the offer and let it be. Eventually, with his help, I earned the money to have one made to my specifications. It was a high-powered 30-06. I own it still.

Twenty-five years later I had the privilege of teaching my own son, Wade, to shoot. Wade was amazing. He had absolutely no fear of firing a weapon but infinite respect for its power. When he was still in high school and we hunted together, I felt safer with him than with anyone else.

In my sophomore and junior years, I played football at Frankfurt High, a small American school in Germany. The highlight of my football career was the banquet after my junior season. My father went with me. Although I was not a first string player, the coach singled me out for effort and courage. My father, in his typical understated way, never said a word about it. Instead, he conveyed his pride by throwing his arm over my shoulders as we walked together after the banquet. I understood his language even then and was thrilled that he was there to witness the recognition of my achievement.

Shortly before I started at Clemson, my father asked if I

intended to play football for the Tigers. I said no. "Good," he said. "College football is a different game from the sport you played in high school." I was a six-foot three-inch, one hundred and forty-five pound bean pole at that time, and my experience was as a defensive tackle! "Tough as you are," he said, "you aren't big enough to go out there and play with those guys."

As serious as my father was, he also had his lighter side. He was even a bit impish at times and would pull your leg with a twinkle in his eye. He played a silly little game with my mother while driving. He would tap out a signal on the steering wheel with a childish grin on his face, and Mother would pull out a cigarette, stick it in her mouth and light it, then pass it to him.

One evening in Germany, my friend Mike and I decided to go out for a few beers. My parents were out already, and we planned to return before they did. I didn't have a key to the house, so I unlocked a window in the back, and we were off. We ended up at a gasthaus that typically was only frequented by German families out for a meal. But that night there was an American soldier at the bar, surrounded by glasses of beer and an earthenware crock of Steinhager. Spurred on by a pretty young woman behind the bar, he had consumed more than enough already and was preparing to leave when he heard us speaking English. He picked up the bottles and placed them on our table. By the time Mike and I stumbled back to the house, my parents were home and the back window was locked. We had no choice but to ring the bell, come what may.

Eventually my father let us in, and I promptly fell flat on my face in the foyer. "Hmmm..." my father said. "I think we have a little problem here." He asked Mike to give him a hand, and they took me up to bed.

Early the next morning, before my father awoke, Mike and I grabbed our shotguns and slipped out of the house to hunt rabbits. Mike told me what had happened, and we speculated what kind of trouble I was in. Then Mike took a shot at a rabbit, and my head exploded in pain. I begged him to unload his gun. We wandered around the woods for the rest of the day, ignoring rabbits and trying to muster the courage to face my father. When I finally met up with him, he looked at me and said, "Son, I don't want to see any repeats of last night." And that was all he ever said about it. That was all he needed to say.

In November of 1954, my freshman year at Clemson, my father suffered a massive heart attack. There was a note taped to my barracks door—Urgent message: Call the dean's office. All I was told then was that my father was in the hospital, and my mother wanted me to come home right away. Someone bought me a ticket and drove me to the airport, and before I knew it I was in Washington. One of my father's military friends met my plane and drove me straight to Ft. Belvoir Army Hospital. When I entered my father's room, he looked up at me through his oxygen tent and asked, "What are you doing here? You need to be in Clemson attending to your classes." Less than an hour later, my father was dead. I didn't expect it, and needless to say I was devastated.

He was buried at Arlington National Cemetery a few days later. The details will never leave me: Taps is being played; I am standing at attention in my cadet uniform, shoes and brass shined to perfection, saluting with tears streaming down my face. I remember that I was greatly embarrassed that I could not model the stoic soldier I knew my father to be. I see now that my shame was unwarranted. I know he would have appreciated my love for him. He would have said, "Decorum be damned."

When I returned to Clemson, I went to the library and researched my father. This man whom I had really known only for the eight years after he returned from combat in WWII, came alive for me on the pages of old newspapers and yearbooks. I read about a young man who was exceptionally active in campus activities. I learned that he was on the staff of *The Tiger*, Clemson's student newspaper; that he was a member of the Jailbird Society, a group that had led a rebellion against perceived injustices at the school and had been locked up for a few days as a result; that, for three years, he played fullback on Clemson's football team. I was struck by the sheer volume of stories about my father, stories that I had never heard. And I realized that my father had been a doer, not a storyteller. Goal-oriented and a high achiever, he had lived his life fully in the present. If I wanted to know about his past, I would have to hear it from others.

While at Clemson, I was fortunate to meet several people who had known my father during his student days there. One day I'll never forget was at the Orange Bowl football game of 1957. A friend and I were leaving breakfast when we ran into several men he knew. After he introduced me, one gentleman asked, "Are you Long John's boy?" I said I was. He immediately stuck out his tongue and said, "Do you see that scar?"

"Yes, sir," I said.

"Your father did that to me," he said. "I was trying to tackle him in practice one day." I stammered an apology on my father's behalf, and the man laughed and asked, "How are you getting to the game, son?" I told him that I had not yet figured that out. He turned to his companion, who had chartered a bus for his friends, and said, "Surely we have room on the bus for Long John's boy and his bride." They did, and for most of the trip they regaled me with stories of my father's exploits as a student and football player.

My father left me with a great legacy; he bequeathed me a moral compass. A man who was constant, irrespective of the situation, he saw his values so clearly that he rarely was caught off guard. Those same values were so clear to others that he rarely was challenged. To this day, I admire my father's values and strive to uphold them. They have served as my foundation—a solid, unwavering point from which to observe and maneuver the sometimes obscure path of life. As you might surmise, he was, and still is, my hero. I had the privilege of naming the John E. Walker, Sr. Golf Course at Clemson University in his honor.

The picture on the right is of my father taken as a US Army infantry colonel a few years before he died.

*Chapter Two*

# THE END JUSTIFIES THE MEANS—OR DOES IT?

It was late afternoon and the eight-man army team waited at the edge of a secluded stand of trees for orders to move out. Earlier, the group of volunteers had been assembled to undertake a covert mission behind enemy lines. The officer in charge had described the mission as critically important. It was imperative that it be completed without detection. If successful, the mission could save thousands of lives.

Final preparation was a buddy check, just before the order was given to move out. Everything appeared to be in order until one of the soldiers began to fidget, stagger, and exhibit signs of severe trauma. Suspecting pre-action panic, the young leader of the mission pulled the soldier aside and tried to calm him down. But things got worse. The unnerved soldier began running aimlessly and making increasingly loud and incoherent sounds. Fearing that the mission would be compromised, the leader acted quickly and decisively, striking him hard with the butt of his rifle. The leader was in the process of assigning two of his men to care for the unconscious soldier when a whistle blew, and the officer in charge informed the volunteers that the mission was cancelled.

The mission, it turns out, was an exercise conducted at Fort Benning, Georgia. Fortunately, all actions, including the rifle butt to the head, were simulated. Unfortunately for the mission leader, the leadership component was deemed less than satisfactory. Unfortunately as well, I was that leader. The army considered my quick willingness to sacrifice the well-being of one of my men unsatisfactory, in spite of mitigating circumstances.

Did my actions that day make me a bad person? I think not. I was an eager young soldier trying to do my job. Did I do a bad thing? Indeed, I did. I allowed the assertion that the mission was critical to goad me, in the pressure of the moment, into acting without adequately considering my options. It was a knee-jerk reaction to an unexpected threat, and, had it not been an exercise, I well might have killed my fellow soldier without a second thought in an attempt to safeguard the mission.

★ ★ ★

A Little League game was in progress. Each team consisted of twelve players, aged nine to twelve. It was the fifth of seven innings. Three dejected boys sat on the bench, as they had since the opening pitch. National Little League rules stated that all players were to play a minimum of two innings per game. The boys on the bench, then, would play the final two innings unless the game was stopped, as they often were, for any one of a number of reasons. For example, there was a time limit on the games; no inning was to start after two hours of play. Or, after the fifth inning, if a team led by ten or more runs at the end of an inning, the game was over.

It is important to note why the three boys were sitting on the bench. Had they been there as a consequence of missing an excessive number of practices or as punishment for bad behavior, it would be a different issue entirely. But the boys simply were not good baseball players. The team manager, wrapped up in the excitement of winning a close game, was leaving his best players on the field. By delaying the weakest players' required play time to the sixth and seventh innings, he was living up to the letter, but not the spirit, of the mandatory rule. Was the manager a bad person? No, he was an enthusiastic coach and a respected member of the community. Did he do a bad thing? Absolutely.

First of all, requiring young players in a developmental league to sit on the bench for five straight innings is just not right. And second, since the game could be called before completing seven innings, the boys could end up playing fewer than two innings. In fact, if time ran out or the score became lopsided, it is possible that they would not play at all. In the excitement of competition, the team manager applied an approach appropriate to adult baseball but not appropriate for a group of youngsters, for whom he had the responsibility of imparting values they would carry into adulthood. Fortunately, while I was affiliated with the league, I was not the team manager.

★ ★ ★

The Reverend Jack Riley appeared haggard and depressed. During morning coffee with a good friend, he confided that, while he was doing everything possible, their church was in poor shape: unsuccessful fundraising had left its finances in deficit; their external ministry goals were not being met because not enough members were volunteering to carry them out; and, most upsetting to him, his relationship with his family was suffering from the excessively long hours he was devoting to the job. He and the lay leadership had unanimously agreed on a set of ministry opportunities that would be sinful to ignore, in spite of any costs the church might incur.

Unfortunately, the well-being of the minister and his

family was one of the prices paid. The minister's wife had recently accused him of spending more time with the children of Haiti than he did with his own children. Furthermore, several families had severed their relationships with the church because they felt unduly pressured to donate time and money to the organization. Would it be fair to call the minister or the lay leadership "bad people?" Indeed not; all were dedicated individuals committing considerable time and effort to making the world a better place. Were bad things happening? Yes. Even the successful realization of the goals they were pursuing would not alter this fact. Unfortunately, even attainment of the goals was far from certain.

Contrast the examples above with the parable at the beginning of the chapter. In each of these stories, the individual suffers for what the decision-maker considers the greater good, while in the parable the entire flock is jeopardized to save the lone lost sheep. I have always found the lost sheep to be one of the most difficult parables in the Bible to understand. To this day, I still ask these questions: Why would someone risk the ninety-nine to potentially save the one? On the other hand, if we are readily willing to sacrifice the one to save the flock, how do we measure the value of the flock? Does it consist simply of expendable sheep? I do not pretend that I have found *the* answers, but the shepherd's way has had a profound impact on my regard for the individual. I have come to believe that it is all too easy to justify the sacrifice of the one for the greater good if the plight of the individual is not factored carefully into the desired outcome.

These stories of good people doing bad things fall into a category that I call "ends and means" situations. Regarding the military leader, the Little League manager, and the minister and lay leadership, it matters little if their actions were well-intentioned. Decisions were made that the anticipated "good" results justified the "bad" means employed to achieve them. Decisions like these are made every day.

- Consider the father who allows his teenage son to ride to a concert with questionable friends because he has been called in to work and "can't" drive the boy as promised.
- Consider the politician who promises to look into a zoning issue that he already knows will not be resolved in his constituents' favor in order to garner votes on an unrelated issue that will benefit the community.
- Consider the salesman who agrees to a delivery date he knows his company cannot meet in order to seal a deal that will satisfy his company's monthly sales goal.
- Consider the church leader who is attempting to fill the critical position of finance committee chair. Knowing that the position is demanding and time-consuming, the leader tells a busy but highly qualified church member, "It will not take much of your time."

Indeed, it is the insidious nature of human desire that inappropriate means are cleverly disguised by the appealing end that beckons. In my experience, there is a strong correlation between the "high calling" of an end—be it in family, business, religion, or social organizations—and the temptation to succumb to inappropriate means. Perhaps it is human nature to be blinded by the vision of achieving something truly worthwhile. After all, who among us would be tempted to use shameful means to achieve "ho-hum" ends? The pitfalls lie in places where the stakes are high.

I believe that people do—sometimes—stand back and deliberate on the ethics of the means they use to achieve a goal. But why, especially among good, moral people, does it not happen more often? Why don't people say, as a matter of course, "I'll be damned if I'll do that!"? In my observation of human behavior, an oft-repeated pattern emerges. People frequently lock onto an outcome, an end, that they deem highly attractive, and then they search for a means to achieve that end. If a goal is decided upon separate from and prior to the actions necessary to achieve that goal, all too often the end is deemed fixed and the means negotiable. It takes strength to challenge a seductive end, to question means—especially convenient ones—that will provide one's heart's desire. It is far easier to forget the unpleasant aspects of a journey in the comfort of the final destination. "The end justifies the means" can be an easy excuse for bad behavior.

Put simply: A blanket acceptance that the end justifies the means is dangerous. It is how, in the extreme, individuals and societies excuse heaping atrocities on our fellow man. It is genocide; it is the Holocaust; it is apartheid. And on a smaller scale, it is how we excuse the tiny atrocities of daily life. Rather than accepting that the end justifies the means, we will only achieve appropriate ends if we live instead by the dictum that it is the end and means together that justify the means.

I have found that if I live by the guideline, "the end never justifies the means," I am seldom inconvenienced and often saved from my own powers of rationalization. I appreciate that, in straightforward situations outside the bounds of morality, a clear and appropriate relationship exists between the means chosen and the desired end. If one wants to nail two boards together, is not the use of a hammer justified? Such deductive reasoning clearly does not require the use of ethical guidelines. But we routinely face more complicated choices. If one wants to nail two boards together, for example, but lacks the wherewithal to buy a hammer, is the theft of one justified? What if someone's life depends on the union of those two boards? As you can see, only tiny steps are required to support the position that the means can be justified by the end, and from there, unfortunately, to the belief that the end *always* justifies the choice of means.

Accordingly, I believe that we must be ever alert to the pitfalls that lie ahead. The means must not be ignored when deciding on an appropriate end or when evaluating the achievement of that end. As an operational guideline, I believe we have no choice but to reject that the end justifies the means. Any problems such a guideline might cause pale in comparison to the potential harms avoided by such a stance.

The penchant to accept an end achieved by inappropriate means can be minimized by the existence of an ethical environment, one that guides decision-makers to look out for the sheep that, for whatever reason, is not in a position to look out for itself. The next chapter will address how pitfalls can be minimized if decisions are made within such an environment. Then, and only then, we are ready to build a firm—or any other organizational entity—with a soul.

*Chapter Three*

# THE SHEPHERD'S WAY

*If a shepherd has a hundred sheep, and one of them goes astray, does he not leave the ninety-nine on the mountains and go in search of the one that went astray?*

(Matthew 18:12, New RSV)

In 1963 I was a first lieutenant on active duty with the United States Army. I was part of a nuclear capable, heavy field artillery battalion stationed close to both the Czechoslovakian and East German borders. I had been serving in Erlangen, Germany, for about a year and a half when the battalion commanding officer called me in and offered me a new assignment. He was a lieutenant colonel, but everyone in the battalion referred to him as the Old Man. While "Old Man" is a common moniker in the army for any officer in charge of a unit, it always struck me how unlike my own "Old Man" he was. My father was perhaps best described as frank in a "rough around the edges" way, while the Old Man of our battalion was spit-and-polish smooth.

The position he offered me that day was the command of one of the battalion's three firing batteries, a unit of approximately one hundred men and considerable responsibility. I was elated. I wanted the position very much. But as I listened to the offer, I realized there was a string attached. As a condition of the new assignment, the Old Man was demanding my complete and unquestioning loyalty to him. I knew that I could not give such blanket assurance, and I told him so. With growing apprehension, I tried to explain my position. "My loyalty lies first with my Creator," I said as respectfully as I could. "Then with humanity, the United States, the US Army, the battalion, and finally, Sir, with you as my commanding officer. If, in the execution of my new command, I were to find myself facing orders that conflicted with my higher duties, I would be required to refuse them."

As I spoke, the Old Man's normally impassive face changed to a frown and then to a look of shocked displeasure. He wasn't used to being told "no," especially by a junior officer. But he quickly regained his balance. "Well," he said in his typical terse manner, "that's just not good enough. I need a higher level of loyalty than that, and since you aren't prepared to give it to me, I'll find an officer who will." And then he dismissed me.

The non-commissioned officers of the battery knew that I was going up to meet with the Old Man. As had I, they thought the job was mine, and they were pulling for me. We had built a close relationship over the past year while I was executive officer of the battery. I knew that, when they found out I had talked my way out of being their new battery commander, they would be almost as disappointed as I was.

After leaving the Old Man's office, I walked around the base trying to let my stomach settle, trying to come to terms with the way things had gone. "It's not such a big deal," I tried telling myself, but I knew that I wanted the position more than any other I would have a chance at during my two-year tour of duty. Even though I had earned my PhD already, which meant that I could easily get assigned to a high-level support branch, I had requested artillery. As an army brat, I believed that the essence of the armed forces was its combat branches. I believed that a combat branch of the army would provide me with decision-making and leadership experience I couldn't get anywhere else in the army. The position I almost had was absolutely perfect in this regard, yet, as I thought about the conditions that came with it, there was no doubt in my mind that I had made the right decision.

Why was I so assertive in this decision compared to the one I made during the military exercise described in the previous chapter? Simply stated, the environment had changed. I now had the benefit of experience and reflection. I had spent a lot of time since the failed mission thinking about why I had behaved badly under pressure. I concluded that, along with inexperience, it was the situation that had skewed my judgment. Accordingly, when faced with my commanding officer's request for unwavering loyalty, I recognized a situation that could place me once again in a potentially compromising position, thus clouding my sense of right and wrong. While this may sound like I had a holier-than-thou sense of duty, I think that is missing the mark. I simply was better prepared this time to make a good decision.

Looking back, I can remember two extraordinary experiences during my college years, experiences that I can now see helped me forge an ethical environment when I found myself challenged to do the right thing. After my father's sudden death, I was beset by uncertainty over my future. I had a nagging feeling that I should follow in my father's footsteps as an army officer. So, after completing my second year at Clemson, I applied for and accepted an appointment to the United States Military Academy at West Point. After about four months at West Point, however, I decided that I had come for the wrong reasons. I really did not want a military career. I applied for a discharge, and, after a month of interviews regarding my motives, it was granted, and I returned to

Clemson.

Although short, my experience at West Point was exceptionally valuable because it introduced me to an environment where honor was stressed above all else. Dishonesty in any form was not tolerated. I recognized my father in the halls of West Point, but I also realized that he had long ago provided me with a moral compass that did not depend on military service to guide me. As much as I respected the outstanding leadership training I would be giving up, I was more interested in intellectual achievement. Resigning was considered shameful, but the honor-based environment at West Point gave me the courage to be honest with myself, accept my mistake, and follow my heart back to Clemson.

Two years later, after graduating Clemson with a BS in industrial management, I enrolled at the University of Virginia to pursue my graduate education. That is where the second extraordinary experience occurred. I knew of UVa's fine academic reputation when I applied to the school, but I was totally unaware that, like West Point, they had an established honor system. Unlike West Point, however, UVa had an honor system that was designed, operated, and enforced by the students. By placing the responsibility of the entire system in the hands of the students, the university had improved upon West Point's approach. UVa's environment included a level of free thinking and freedom that allowed each student to take ownership of his behavior. When I first helped administer an exam, I was informed by the professor that exams were not proctored at UVa. My only job was to be available to answer questions. The students were on their honor to abide by the rules. I received a fine education at the University of Virginia and had the pleasure of studying under a great faculty, two of whom were subsequently awarded The Nobel Prize in economics, but what I remember most about my time there is having been part of an environment of honor.

I did not entirely recognize it when I was in college or when I refused my commanding officer's condition of unquestioning loyalty, but I have learned from a lifetime of such experiences to appreciate *an established moral environment* as a necessary condition to sound decision-making. In fact, I believe it is virtually impossible to overestimate the importance of a moral environment when making decisions. Had I accepted command of the artillery battery, along with the strings, I would have placed myself in a situation where my freedom to act ethically might have been severely curtailed. Even worse, without prior understanding of what is now referred to as the "rules of engagement," I could have been required to do something I would end up regretting for the rest of my life.

The Erlangen story, however, has a happy ending. About four days after our first meeting, the Old Man called me back into his office. He sat behind his desk looking depressed and annoyed. After a long, uncomfortable silence, he said, "Lieutenant Walker, I believe this is the worst day of my life." And then he gave me the assignment—no strings attached. I think he saw the decision as a humiliating defeat. Actually, I respected him for taking the difficult road. The situation at the battalion at the time was such that he did not have a good alternative to giving me the assignment. We had few officers who could fill the position, and whether he liked me or not he knew I soldiered hard and would do the job well.

What could have been a personal disappointment and a career set-back turned out to be the best period of my military life, and one of the most satisfying periods of my life in general. While the Old Man never warmed up to me, he did allow me to do my job free from inappropriate constraints. I was able to apply my own beliefs and training to the benefit of the men under my command. Although I did not yet think of it in such terms, I had established an ethical environment, one that treated the men with respect and in turn inspired initiative and honest, hard work on their part. The resulting superior performance of the battery benefited everyone, including my commanding officer.

The baseball situation discussed in Chapter Two was resolved by changing the rules for the local Little League. In one of our monthly board meetings, I proposed that the minimum number of innings be changed from two to four. Immediately, one of the most experienced and respected managers turned red. He stood up and got in my face. "Don't you trust us?" he bellowed.

After recovering from the shock of the challenge, I said, "No. I don't. I don't trust myself, for that matter, in the midst of the thrill of competition, to always properly discharge my responsibility to the players." I went on to explain that I thought we needed to place constraints that would level the playing field for all coaches and provide a clear statement of what we stood for. The motion was unanimously passed. We created a *moral environment* that compelled all the managers to do the right thing, thus freeing them to be the best coaches they could be.

The example of the Reverend Jack Riley and his church cited in Chapter Two illustrates how an unhealthy environment can be created by good intentions. Recall the statement: "He and the lay leadership had unanimously agreed on a set of ministry opportunities that would be sinful to ignore, in spite of any costs the church might incur."

While well-intentioned, this position created an environment conducive to the pursuit of lofty goals at the expense of the human and monetary resources of the church. In contrast, imagine a church with leadership that creates a *moral environment* for its congregation; an environment that focuses on helping its members discover and apply their talents rather than focusing on an imperative to do good works with no consideration of the human cost.

Essentially, there are two approaches an individual can take to avoid falling victim to the lure of the glorified end. The more basic and probably more difficult approach is for a person to build such strength of character that temptation is virtually nonexistent. This was my father's approach, and for the most part it worked to protect him from doing bad things to achieve good ends. In the other approach, the individual places himself in an environment that condones and promotes ethical behavior. While more complex, the environmental approach is undoubtedly more often successful because it gives the individual the strength of the community. This approach has been enormously successful at Andesa, and I will address its application to the firm in more detail later.

A combination of the two approaches—a highly ethical individual in an environment that fully supports ethical choices—clearly is the best of both worlds. Obviously all individuals and environments are on an ethical spectrum, none being totally good or totally bad. Perfection, while something to strive for, is not a requirement. It is the intention and propensity to do the right thing that make up an ethical individual or environment.

It is easy to use the term "ethical" or "moral" or "good" and assume that the meaning is clear, and for the most part it probably is. We all know right from wrong, good from bad. We could sit down and make a list of core values that pretty much transcend religion, culture, and society. But that doesn't stop most of us, in moments of weakness, from excusing bad behavior when pursuing a lofty goal. In order to highlight some important aspects of the environment as it pertains to the "end and means" situation, I will take a moment here to discuss specific characteristics of an ethical environment that I think were so important in the building of Andesa.

**Respect.** In an ethical environment, the individual

is respected. In order for management to succeed in guiding people toward good decision-making, the environment must have the well-being of its people at its core. Employees must trust their managers and co-workers to stand behind them. People must believe this respect to be honest respect, not a ruse aimed at manipulating them. For example, the employees of Andesa say they are motivated to work hard because they believe that the firm cares about them as whole people, not just as employees. They feel as though they mean something to the firm, and in turn the firm means more than a paycheck to them. It is important to note that the creation of an insincerely caring environment designed solely to achieve greater productivity would reek of manipulation and would quickly lead to a loss of faith in the organization.

**Honesty.** In an ethical environment not only are people honestly respected, honesty is valued above all else. The culture focuses on honesty, not because it will bring a profit or please the client, but simply and solely because it is the right thing to do. The individual is given great power in an environment where people are expected to be honest. The subterfuge of turning a blind eye to lying, cheating, stealing, trickery, or any other kind of dishonesty in the name of attaining a goal effectively undermines the individual's desire to do good by creating competing loyalties. Alternatively, in an environment that sincerely promotes honesty, the individual is free to be truthful, even if the truth may have costs for the organization. A hard truth, by definition, is not easy. It is the man reporting the whereabouts of his dangerous brother to the authorities. It is the coach giving his new quarterback time on the field, possibly losing the game, because he promised the young man that he would play.

It is the new data entry personnel going to her boss and admitting that she just deleted three days of records, even if the error could not be traced back to her. Within a supportive environment, doing the right thing still may not be easy, but it is respected.

**Trust.** In an ethical environment, people are trusted. They are trusted to express their thoughts. They are trusted to work hard and do the right thing without constant supervision. By extension, this freedom to act means that the individual is free to succeed and free to fail. While avoidance of careless failure is obviously important in any organization, an environment that provokes widespread fear of failure in both actions and ideas is disastrous to the individual's confidence and willingness to take initiative.

**Initiative.** Initiative is valued in an ethical environment. It encourages people to live up to their potential. And while it is good for an organization when its people excel, it is equally beneficial to the individual. Personal growth and satisfaction are common results of a job well done. In an environment that rewards hard work, initiative, and willingness to accept responsibility, management will seldom need to correct for shirking or failure to do one's job.

**Courage.** In an ethical environment, courage is promoted. The firm stands behind its people in the hard choices they make. And courage is vital in the decision-making process because the glorified end has a way of making even the most black and white decision difficult. But when you know that you will be backed up by those around you, even the hardest choices and actions become doable.

An environment with these core values affirms the worth of the individual and frees employees from undue and conflicting pressures to justify questionable means. It encourages thinking over blind obedience and rewards initiative and willingness to accept responsibility. People rise to the occasion in such an environment. They create and nurture a firm with a soul. It is the Shepherd's way—frequently difficult, always rewarding.

*Chapter Four*

# THE NATURE OF THE FIRM[1]

When my tour of duty ended in the summer of 1963, I returned to the United States with my wife and son to begin a new job with the Research Triangle Institute in North Carolina. I had been a student and a soldier, and now it was time for me to transition into the business world. And likewise, it is time now in my story to turn the discussion of the ethical environment to the business world, to the firm in particular, where, without a doubt, it belongs but often does not occupy the position of importance it deserves.

In order to best understand the role of ethics in the environment and operation of the firm, it is helpful to consider the following question: Why does the firm exist? I have discussed this question with business owners and managers, politicians at various levels of government, professionals in many fields, and fellow economists. Some think of the firm in terms of what it produces. In other words, they believe it exists simply to manufacture some product or service. Others think of the firm in terms of job creation. A third group thinks of the firm as an instrument to generate profits for its investors. While all of these ways of understanding the firm are valid,

---

[1] Coase, Ronald H. "The Nature of the Firm." *Economica* (November 1937), 4(16).

each approaches the firm from its own unique perspective: the consumer, the employee, and the investor.

There is a final group, the academics, who typically meld those definitions to include a broader perspective, one that more fully describes the nature of the firm. Today's economist, for example, thinks of the firm as a nexus of contracts creating an organization that coordinates the processes of production and distribution. This definition, as I will explain later in the chapter, brings us closest to the way of thinking about the firm that I want to propose as necessary to creating a firm with a soul.

I feel fortunate to have been trained as an economist, and I must admit that it was not my own initiative that led me down that path. It never would have happened, in fact, but for the efforts of an economics professor I encountered in undergraduate school. Professor Hugh H. Macaulay was a long-time professor of economics at Clemson. He so loved his subject that many students in his class were eventually infected with a love of economics. It could not be helped. He created an environment within which even the least motivated of his students benefited. His obvious enthusiasm inspired us to explore and understand the material. His presentations sparkled. He approached topics with genuine excitement and

The picture on the right is of Hugh Macaulay courtesy of his family.

would ask rhetorically, "Is it true that if the price of a good is lowered, fewer units of the good might be sold?" And then after a pause he would say, "Yea, verily. That might be so. Even though buyers may want more, the seller may want to sell less at a lower price." His demeanor drew us to try to discover what about economics could so excite this great teacher. At the time I did not think in terms of environment, but I now understand that he was a master of creating an environment of learning. He believed in his students; he challenged us, and in this environment we flourished. I now see that environment as a monument to his passion for his students.

Hugh Macaulay personally touched my life in my senior year at Clemson. One day he invited me to his office, as he did now and then with all his students. "Mr. Walker," he said, "what are your plans for graduate school?"

Flabbergasted, I said, "Professor Macaulay, I don't have any plans." The truth be known, I was tired of formal schooling.

"Mr. Walker," he stated, "you belong in graduate school. You have an aptitude for learning." And just like that everything changed—my attitude, my motivation, and my belief in my academic ability. It was almost like I *had* to change. What cad would not respond to such interest from the master? The magic of Hugh Macaulay was evidenced months later when I was admitted to the graduate program in economics at the University of Virginia, with a smile on my face; yea, verily.

Because I am trained as an economist and because the modern economist spends a great deal of time considering the purpose of the firm, I believe that a brief summary of the history of economic thought on the firm will help the reader understand how we think of the firm today.

Historically, the firm was thought of as what is now known as the black box: an organization that buys inputs, converts them to outputs, and sells them as new products. By focusing solely on what the firm produces for the marketplace, the black box approach ignores the fundamental issue of why people organize into firms in the first place, rather than create products as individuals.

In 1937, Ronald Coase addressed the issue by inviting the academic community to pierce the veil and look inside that black box. In his groundbreaking article, "The Nature of the Firm," Coase introduced the concept of transaction costs as the economic rationale for the firm. He argued that the high cost of coordinating resources through the marketplace when manufacturing a product or service leads to the formation of the firm as a means of reducing these costs. In other words, it is not the production of a good or service that compels people to organize, but rather it is the relatively high cost of doing it alone.

According to Coase, the essence of the firm is the arrangement whereby owners of the factors of production delegate to the firm's managers the power to make decisions with respect to the use of these resources. All parties expect to benefit from this arrangement, and those benefits are typically thought of in financial terms.

I want to note here that benefits are much more than a higher salary or a better health insurance package. Quality of life, vacation time, and a clear conscience, are three potential benefits that come to mind outside the financial realm. When I discuss benefits later in this book, I am including the more complex issues of human resources along with more traditional monetary benefits.

I studied under Professor Coase in the early 1960s while working on my PhD in economics at UVa. My specialty was microeconomic theory, known also as price theory or the study of how individuals and firms interact in the marketplace. We were studying the firm, but even in Professor Coase's class it was the role of price in the allocation of resources that was the key focus. The internal workings of the firm were yet to be of much interest.

Eventually, economists accepted Coase's invitation to look

inside the firm, and his seminal definition of the firm led to the creation of an entire sub-discipline of economics that explores the nature of the firm.

In their 1972 paper, *Production, Information Costs, and Economic Organization*,[2] Armen Alchian and Harold Demsetz go a step further in describing the human relationships of an organization rather than the marketplace products. They speak of the firm in terms of interdependency. As much as the worker is an employee of the manager, they assert, the manager is an employee of the worker. One is hired to be a member of a team of workers; the other to make sure each employee does his job. The purpose of the firm is to take advantage of the interdependence of the productivity of each worker in a team environment. This interdependence is well-illustrated with respect to the members of a football team. If each does his job, the team has a good chance to reach its goal of scoring a touchdown. Two things are important to note about team production. First, the product (in this case a touchdown) is more than any member could achieve alone, and second, the failure of any one member to do his job can readily negate the work of the entire team. This is the nature of team production, and according to Alchian and Demsetz, it is one of the important rationales for the existence of the firm.

Michael Jensen and Bill Meckling followed in 1976 with "Theory of the firm: Managerial behavior, agency costs, and ownership structure."[3] Theirs is the "nexus of contracts" definition mentioned above. To repeat, a firm is a nexus of contracts creating an organization that coordinates the processes of production and distribution.

The nexus of contracts Jensen and Meckling discuss are the written contracts between employees and managers, the firm and its clients, and suppliers and the firm. They are the formal

---

[2] *American Economic Review*, (December) 62(5), pp. 777–95.

3 *Journal of Financial Economics*, (October) 3(4), pp. 305–360.

agreements that facilitate transactions and team interaction and explain the complex interactions between equity and debt holders. Their important work strongly emphasized individual incentives, agency costs, and monitoring and measuring behavior. Not surprisingly, it sparked significant study of the complexity that we so simply call "the firm." This is basically where we stand today in economic thought on the purpose of the firm.

The firm is a complex set of interconnected contracts between workers, managers, owners, suppliers, and ultimately buyers. But consider the other contracts that exist between the people involved with a firm. The handshake between a manager and a new employee that says "I will treat you right" and "I will work hard for the company." The honest timeline the client services rep gives a new client, and the subsequent faith the client puts in the firm by giving it a chance to fix a mistake. In essence, values are contracts, and ethical behavior is a contract. These implicit contracts, as much or more than the formal ones, are why I believe the firm exists.

For example, Andesa enters into formal contracts with its clients to provide services in accordance with a Statement of Work. Our pricing structure is included in this written contract. Understandably, the client is typically concerned about cost; they want to pay as little as possible. Andesa understands this. We also know that, when clients contract for services, they are relying on the assumption that we will continue in business for many years. So at the contracting stage, we engage clients in a critical discussion of our pricing structure and philosophy. We explain why our ongoing costs initially are relatively low but are indexed to inflation because, ultimately, we will cease to exist if we can no longer provide our services profitably. Occasionally, companies price for short-run gains and go out of business or discontinue services as soon as they stop making money. We do not consider that approach honest or fair, and we tell our clients that it is in our joint interest that we remain profitable. Typically, they agree.

We do not try to reduce this critical discussion of how we do business to a formal contract. Rather, we build an informal contract together as we agree on a business philosophy of honesty and mutual respect.

At this point, I propose an employee-centered definition of the firm that acknowledges the role of ethics:

> The firm exists to provide an ethical environment in which employees can fully develop and apply their business skills, in order to benefit the employee, the client, and the shareholder.[4]

Let us examine more closely the proposed definition and its implications. The *imperative* is for the firm to provide an ethical environment for its employees. In this regard, I believe I am in full agreement with modern economic thought, from Coase onward. If the firm exists to reduce transaction costs by creating a nexus of contracts among individuals, it is to a large measure this culture of ethics that allows for it. Ethics are rules of engagement, so to speak. They are the universal standard for interaction between individuals. Specifically, in the case of the firm, ethics is the basis for interdependency, for working together to create something that cannot be created alone.

But why do I focus on the employee? Why not the traditional land, labor, and capital of economics? The employee plays the unique role of change agent in the firm. It is the employee's activities that takes the factors of production and effectively utilizes them to create benefits for the client and profits for the shareholder. Until employees become involved, we merely have the raw ingredients. The firm serves the client and the shareholder through the employee.

Up to this point, I have been discussing the firm in terms of

---

[4] I use the term shareholder to mean an equity shareholder or stockholder.

positive economics. I have been talking about descriptions of what the firm is, not what it should be. Now I will shift from economic theory and address the reality of an imperfect world. We know that no institution, including the firm, is perfect. We know that firms fail to varying degrees to provide an ethical environment for their employees. My position is that the firm *should* engage in a nexus of implicit contracts that are ethical and focused on the good of the individual. It *should* adopt as its vision statement my employee-centered definition of the firm. Apart from whether it makes good business sense, it *should* do this because it is the right thing to do.

This imperative is not something I created. I have simply identified it, formalized it within the context of the firm. From a broader perspective, ethical behavior is the nature of the society in which we live. It is the humanist telling us that people are special and should be so treated. It is the priest, the rabbi, the imam, or the monk telling us people are holy and should be so treated. It is your mother telling you to be nice to your little sister. There are rules dictating how we treat one another. Why, merely because the context is the marketplace, would it be acceptable for the rules to cease to apply in the firm? I suggest that they do apply, and when they are followed, the firm, the individual, and society are all better off.

Interestingly enough, if a firm operates ethically, it will create an environment in which each and every person who enters into a relationship with the firm stands to benefit. And this is the beauty of the firm. It takes us right back into the realm of positive economics. When an ethical environment allows the employees of a firm to thrive, the clients benefit and the shareholders benefit, and in turn the firm has its very best chance to succeed in the marketplace.

*Chapter Five*

# APPLICATION OF ETHICS TO THE FIRM

A human being who lacks a sense of moral responsibility or social conscience is called a sociopath. All one must do is imagine the infamous fictional sociopath, Hannibal Lecter, to know without a doubt the importance of a soul. And then consider why it should be any different for a firm. Imagine the havoc a firm without a social conscience, without empathy for the individual, could create in society.

We know how a person distinguishes between right and wrong, but how does a firm, a jumble of implicit and explicit contracts between sometimes thousands of diverse and ever-changing employees, know right from wrong? And what makes it choose one over the other? How does the firm develop a sense of moral responsibility? How does it protect the individual?

Consider four alternative policies that a firm may pursue in assuring the well-being of the individuals who work for it.

- A firm can treat its employees as assets. It follows that the firm will then protect those assets.

- A firm can employ ethical managers who give priority to the ethical treatment of its employees.

- A firm can rely on and abide by regulations that mandate the ethical treatment of its employees.

- And, finally, a firm can integrate into its culture the standard that employees be treated ethically.

While none of the above approaches is harmful to the employee, per se, each, apart from the last, has pitfalls that make it less than acceptable as an overall approach to protecting the individual.

The inherent flaw of the first alternative is that the policy implies that employees are *merely* assets, no different from the firms' computers, copiers, or office space, and, as such, it is to the benefit of the firm to care for them. Just as the firm services its copiers and purchases virus protection for its computers, this approach suggests that the firm cares for its employees so they will continue to perform. This is tantamount to saying that I *treat* you well *only* because you do something for me. In fact, the asset approach subtly guides management to think of employees only in terms of the benefits they bring to the firm. It fails to convey to the employee the message that she is valued as a whole person. And when respect for the individual is lost, so too are the other core values that form the basis for implicit contracts.

Alternative two falls short simply because, as noted in Chapter Two, well-meaning people can do bad things. If the environment is conducive to focusing on the end instead of the end and means as a whole, the temptation to gloss over the steps taken to a goal is often enough to elicit bad behavior from otherwise decent people.

The difficulty with alternative three, as history has shown, is that regulation can never replace ethical behavior. People don't typically like to be regulated, and thus regulation elicits behavior that may conform to the letter, but not the spirit, of the regulation. The US Tax Code is a case in point. Tax evasion is illegal, but tax avoidance is expected. Safe harbors exist throughout the Code. They, in effect, state, *if your actions fall within prescribed limits, you will be in compliance with the Code whether or not you are abiding by the spirit of the Code.* When it comes to the speed limit, the general attitude is, "Break it if you can get away with it."

Alternative four rises above the others because it is the most constant. It has the benefit of having multiple built-in safeguards. The ethical treatment of employees, if embedded in the culture of the firm, is subject to neither change by personnel nor interpretation by the vagaries of specific situations. If a firm does the right thing even if nobody is looking, it stops wasting time and resources searching for moments when the coast is clear. It stops spending effort creating smoke screens and slights of hand. It just does the right thing. Keep in mind that "the right thing" is sometimes subjective, and well-meaning individuals make errors in judgment. An ethical environment is not a foolproof means of protecting the individual, but it is the most comprehensive approach in a world of fallible human beings.

It is important to note that the first three of these approaches are not bad—just incomplete. And because of what they lack, each fails to ensure the good treatment of its employees. Employees cannot be harmed by being treated like assets, nor can they suffer from the presence of an ethical manager or from compliance to human resource regulations. But if the firm assumes that it is immune to bad behavior because it follows one of the first three approaches instead of cultivating an ethical environment, it is destined to fail the individual. There are just too many temptations in the world.

Let's look at what an ethical environment does when it is integrated into the culture of a firm. An ethical environment is a positive addition to any organization, and a firm is no exception. The environment, good or bad, has a significant and lasting effect on everyone associated with it. It is not surprising, then, that it has the greatest effect on the people most continually exposed to it: the employees. So I will begin with a discussion of some of the ways the environment affects the employee.

The ethical environment encourages and facilitates the personal and professional growth of the firm's employees. When a firm trusts its employees, it gives them the freedom to make decisions, take chances, and follow their instincts in problem-solving. This translates into boundless opportunities for growth, learning, and exploration. When a firm respects its employees, it treats them with dignity when they fail and uses mistakes as opportunities for learning and growing. It holds them to a high standard, but always gives them the support to meet that standard. A firm that takes responsibility for its employees does everything in its power to have the resources available to help them succeed both in their jobs and their lives.

An ethical environment dramatically reduces abuse of the employee. For example, if the golden rule is one of the implicit contracts of the firm, the effect of any action on an individual will be considered. Decisions will not be made separate and apart from the well-being of the people they affect. A new client or project may be postponed when employees are already overworked. Or employees may be asked to work overtime for a period of expanded demand rather than hire an employee whom the firm will be forced to let go when the workload returns to normal. Also, when a firm does not ever ask for or abide by unethical behavior, a standard of doing the right thing is set. Employees don't have to worry about subtle pressure from above to cut corners or tell lies for the good of the company. Decent people who are continually expected to act badly in the name of the company tend to become disheartened, disenfranchised, and disgruntled.

The presence of an ethical environment does not mean that expectations of employee effort will not occasionally be too high. Nor does it mean that employees will never be encouraged to expend their efforts beyond what reasonably should be expected in order to meet a client's needs. The real world is not perfect: management fails to properly plan; clients expect more than agreed upon; markets swing; employees get sick; and on and on. In this respect, however, any shortfalls in the environment provided for employees should be short-term aberrations, not the modus operandi.

In addition to providing opportunity, growth, and decent treatment, an ethical environment promotes a sense of responsibility in its employees. An employee who is treated well by his firm is likely, in return, to take ownership of the work he does and care about the well-being of the firm. Industriousness is often a byproduct of a culture where hard work is expected and rewarded. A willingness to work hard for the firm's success translates into a team mentality that inspires employees to sacrifice time, emotion, and effort when the good of the firm requires it.

Both the firm and any potential employee should be aware of the responsibility and industriousness required of employees in an ethical environment. Someone who finds this responsibility unattractive, someone who simply wants to show up and collect a paycheck, should probably seek out a firm with a low-expectation environment. I have found, however, that most people have higher expectations of themselves and will embrace both the opportunities and the obligations of being part of an ethical firm.

An obvious question at this point is: Is it appropriate for the firm to create such an environment? Some may argue that it is beyond the purview of the firm to so encourage, facilitate, and expect the best effort of the employee in return. This position, however, ignores both the special role the firm plays within society and the productivity of fulfillment. First, whether we like it or not, the firm is a huge part of any working individual's existence and as such should be a healthy, positive place. And second, fulfilled employees are better employees, and it is the essence of good management to bring out the very best in the people they manage. When good leadership encourages and facilitates rather than pushes and dictates, everyone wins. When an employee is passionate about his job rather than going through the motions, everyone wins.

## A Word about Clients and Shareholders

Up to this point, I have focused on the ethical treatment of the employee as the primary focus of the firm. But it is important to point out that the ethical environment does not stop at the employee; it applies to any entity associated with the firm. While the employee is the most directly affected by the environment, be it good or bad, the firm has a responsibility to both the shareholder and the client as well to treat them by the same ethical standard.

"The customer is always right." "The client is king." In today's vernacular, it is certainly true that the client is the center of the universe. This idea is both appealing and widely advocated in today's service-oriented world. But if the client is considered in terms of the firm's ethical environment, I would propose that the client be treated rather differently. I would propose that, as with the employee, the client be treated ethically. When using a moral standard, the client is entitled to respect, honesty, and industriousness, not a crown of gold or a throne to sit upon. In the business world, this translates into fair prices, honored delivery dates, agreed-upon quality, care and concern about their business, etc. Clients who appreciate the firm's efforts on their behalf, and reciprocate, will help create a culture of mutual respect that motivates both the firm's management and its employees.

To say the client is always right is fraught with the potential for abuse of both the client and the employee. It follows, if the client is always right, that the employee is wrong even if she is right and the client is right even if she is wrong. This logic is dishonest and disrespectful of both the employee and the client, and it leads to a level of interaction that is patronizing at best. Imagine instead the good that can come from rising above right and wrong to a place where a problem can be solved, a mistake corrected.

Consider the shareholder. Is the purpose of the firm to make money for the shareholder? Is the shareholder entitled to a particular return on his investment? I think not. True, the shareholder provides financial resources to the firm in expectation of a return. However, the shareholder is not entitled to a return at the expense of the firm's employees or clients but rather is entitled to the *profits* of the firm, large or small, after the firm has discharged its other responsibilities. Again, if the relationship is regarded in terms of an ethical environment, the firm has the responsibility to be a good steward of the shareholder's investments and to work ethically to make the firm as good as it can be. If the firm keeps its priorities straight and respects its employees, profits will likely come and ultimately the shareholder will benefit.

I cannot overemphasize the point that, while a firm is likely to reap more profits for its shareholders and better serve its clients if it creates an ethical environment for its employees, these are *not* the fundamental reasons for establishing such an environment. Whereas I hope and believe that all parties will benefit from such a culture, I promote ethics in the workplace because treating employees ethically is simply the right thing to do. If the firm embraces ethics solely as a recipe for financial success, it risks becoming manipulative rather than honest and respectful. Doing the right thing cannot be reserved for times when it is convenient or free. A firm must be so committed to conducting itself in an ethical manner that it is willing to fail in the marketplace if necessary in order to maintain its good name.

This is not to say, however, that the client and the shareholder *must not* benefit. Financial success is and should be a prominent goal of any firm, but it shouldn't be its moral code. With respect to Andesa, this has indeed been the case.

But how does all this translate to the real world? Is the creation of an ethical environment to serve as the foundation of the firm a realistic goal? In the next three chapters, I am pleased to present the story of the real world firm Andesa Services, Inc. as a resounding "yes."

*Chapter Six*

# The Birth of Andesa

The fiery little firm now known as Andesa Services, Inc. has been around for over twenty-five years. Initially part of Covert and Associates, Inc., it became the third party administration component of The Andesa Companies, Inc. in 1982 when the company was renamed. In 1989 it became a separate entity known as Andesa TPA, Inc. The name was changed a final time in 2004 to reflect the firm's broader span of services offered.[1]

To truly understand Andesa, however, it is necessary to go back much farther than its inception; hence the stories of my father and my time in the army. In fact, I feel as though much of my early life was in preparation for Andesa Services, Inc. Looking back, I can see my gradual progression toward understanding the importance of an ethical environment in any organization and the courage to take a stand against excuses for its absence, particularly in the business world. But it wasn't until 1978, a cool spring night in the middle of May, that I took my first tangible steps in Andesa's direction. My first wife, Ruth, my best friends, Barry and Louise Young, and I went to dinner at the home of our friends Mac and Becky Briggs to discuss an employment opportunity, and the next day I found myself

---

[1] Throughout this series of name changes, the entity remained the same. Thus I shall use the name "Andesa" to represent the firm, regardless of the period.

embarking on a career in which I could test my convictions.

A year earlier, the founder of Covert and Associates, Inc. (CTA), an insurance-driven, executive counseling and benefits company, had approached me to consult on a serious technical problem they were facing. Hal Covert and I discussed his company, several complex issues they were struggling with, and what type of person he would need to tackle those issues. Several times he hinted that he thought I could do the job well, but each time I re-routed the conversation. I wasn't intrigued by the problem as he spelled it out, and at that time in my life I was looking for a job that promised fulfillment. I did not want him to make an offer I would summarily decline.

Nearly a year after my meeting with Hal, Mac Briggs asked me to reconsider the position. Mac was a senior employee at CTA, and he was surprised when I told him that I had not been formally offered a position with the company, that I had in fact worked hard to avoid the offer. "Just hear me out," he said. "Give me a chance to change your mind." At the time, I was an associate professor of economics and Director of the Computing Center at Lehigh University. I had taken the teaching position in 1967, expecting to stay at Lehigh for three to five years before moving on to another university. I was now completing my eleventh year at Lehigh and had decided that it was time to leave academia. At one time, I dreamed of becoming a university president, but Dr. James Schlesinger had convinced me to rethink that goal. A former professor of mine at the University of Virginia and former US Secretary of Defense, Dr. Schlesinger, had come to Lehigh to participate in a foreign policy colloquium. During his visit, I asked him if he would consider running a university now that he was no longer in government. He seemed especially qualified for the position. Upon hearing my question he looked at me as though I were daft and said, "Do I look like a masochist? I know of no job with more responsibility and less authority than that of a university president."

Although I was looking around for something outside of academia that I could develop a real passion for, the position at CTA sounded more like a lost cause than an opportunity for fulfillment. In fact, I agreed to reconsider it simply because of Mac's involvement with the company. Mac and I had served on the Lehigh Valley Young Life Committee together for the past couple of years, and I had come to appreciate and respect his values. I was concerned about the problems he was facing; thus, the dinner meeting.

The six of us spent the evening discussing the company. We rehashed the technical problems Hal Covert had highlighted in our conversation the year before, and then we moved on to the bigger picture. We talked at length about the firm's people, and it occurred to me as the evening progressed that CTA's problems were not technical; they were people-based. As best as I could determine, there were opposing factions at CTA that had dramatically differing views of how the company should be operated. The company's own people were working against each other. Early in my career, I had been interested almost solely in technical problems, but my experience in the army had forced me to deal with personnel management issues. The more time and energy I devoted to exploring people issues, the more they intrigued me. Once I understood the nature of the problems at CTA, my interest was piqued.

At the end of the evening, we piled in the car and headed home. Not once during our get-together had anyone asked if I was going to take the job. On the way home, however, Barry said, "Well? What do you think?"

To my own surprise, I answered, "I'm definitely considering it, but I'm not sure why."

Louise, from the back seat, said, "This is not the John Walker I know. Don't you require all the i's to be dotted and the t's crossed up front?" Louise is a penetrating person who is comfortable asking the difficult questions. What she said was true, and I was having a hard time answering her.

Before I could answer, Barry asked, "Do you feel at peace about this?"

I liked that question better. "I really do," I said. "Again, I don't know why, but I have a feeling this may be the place for me." They all chimed in then. They could see that I was at peace, they said.

I asked them, "If I told you that I was going to accept the position, what would you say?" One at a time, they assured me that they would fully support my decision. The next morning I called Mac and asked him to have Hal Covert send me a formal offer.

The primary business of CTA was financial counseling of executives and the design and operation of supplemental benefit plans to meet their needs. I felt qualified for the job. But because of their internal problems, I went to work at CTA expecting that I would be in deep water, that I could be, in fact, in over my head. I would be forced to either swim like the devil or drown. Surprisingly, I found the challenge exhilarating. My father had never backed away from a challenge, and I suspect that he would have relished this challenge as well. Was I beginning to follow in his footsteps? Prior to joining CTA, I had given my best in every position I held, and I believe I always did a good job. I liked challenges but wasn't a gambler; I stuck with jobs I knew I liked, jobs I knew I could handle. But, somehow, this was going to be different. I sensed it; I sensed that I would have the opportunity to do significant things, even if I didn't know yet what those things would be. In today's parlance, I perceived an opportunity to move the company from good to great.[2]

I joined CTA in August 1978, as a senior member of the management team, which consisted at the time of Hal Covert, Mac Briggs, Bob Rust, Bob Vanduzer, and Greg Confair. Initially, I was hired to construct executive benefits models, and my first year with the firm was unexpectedly calm. I hired Mike Brichta to assist me in computer programming. Together we did interesting work, which culminated in the building of a Monte Carlo simulation model that clearly portrayed the uncertain consequences of retirement decisions. Nothing earth-shattering, but it was an interesting application of skills I had already acquired. Independent of his work skills, Mike was a significant addition to the environment. He had learned healthy time-management skills at home and at college, where he juggled the conflicting demands of being a student-athlete. He was well regarded by all, in part because he never had the talent, time, or patience for office politics.

Partway through my first year at CTA, I was made a member of the Board of Directors and COO of the company. I continued my work as an analyst and turned part of my focus to personnel, which was now one of my official responsibilities. As I began addressing some of the firm's personnel issues, I came to believe that the crux of the problem was the environment. To put it bluntly, CTA was dysfunctional. Essentially, two groups existed and oft times neither felt inclined to try to understand the other, much less find common ground on which to work together to solve problems. Too many people were addressing tasks with too little guidance. This led to some important matters being ignored, while others had people stepping on

---

[2] The phrase "good to great" belongs to Jim Collins. You will find a wonderful exploration of what it takes to move a company from good to great in his book by that title. Harper Business, 2001.

each other's toes to address them.

By this time, I was beginning to have a grasp on CTA's problems. Although I did not fully understand why, I could see that the company was proceeding without real direction. A common approach to a task was to begin work before the objective was properly defined. Indeed, it is hard work to rigorously define an objective; impossible, in fact, if management does not recognize the need to do so. This was frequently the case at CTA, and the absence of clear operational goals (ends) led naturally to a lot of wasted time and effort. Much of the work done during this time (means) was, at best, the employee's guess as to what task was meant to be accomplished. Consequently, results often proved of little or no value to the manager assigning the task. In many of the areas of the company, this lack of guidance led to employees being deprived of the opportunity for recognition of a job well done. This is not to say that CTA's employees weren't working hard. Oftentimes, they were. Rather, because of the environment, they were not doing their jobs well. It may not be obvious that that this environment creates ethical issues, but it does. Allowing a person to waste their time for lack of proper guidance simply is wrong and violates the Golden Rule. Like the parable of the lost sheep, I believed we at CTA were challenged to be conscious of the impact of the workplace on the welfare of each individual. For me, the parable meant addressing directly the sticky area of ends and means.

In writing this book, I have thought a lot about when and how I began addressing CTA's unhealthy environment. I had all but convinced myself that, in name at least, the idea of the employee-centric, ethical environment had come much later in the development of Andesa. I imagined that at some point I put a name to something my partners and I developed somewhat haphazardly over the years to address various ethical issues. But then, while reviewing early corporate records, I uncovered a handwritten document dated October 10, 1979, in which I state that "the purpose of CTA is to provide an environment for the growth of employees." Honestly, I was surprised. My definition of the firm was formulated in Andesa's infancy. In fact, of course, the process began once again with my father. As a child, I had watched him more than once jeopardize his career rather than place people in bad situations. His early death denied me the opportunity to discuss with him his underlying philosophy, but that was his style anyway. Through his actions, my father had given me the concept of an ethical environment, but it was my responsibility to find the words to articulate it.

The 1979 document was followed by a twenty-four page handout for the Board of Directors' 1980 fall retreat. In it I state that:

> Covert and Associates exists to provide its employees an environment for their growth. Employees, in one sense, the traditional sense, are a means to an end. The end is the product provided the customer and the employee is merely one of the resources used to produce that product. At one level of thinking, this relationship certainly is true. At another level, however, this definition is both offensive and dangerous. Offensive because people are more than machines and should not be treated as the same at any level (definitional or otherwise). Dangerous because once people can be thought of on the level of machines, transition to treating them as such can be deceptively easy.

This focus on the well-being of the employee is what I mean by the term "employee-centric." Such an environment is ripe with support, respect, challenge, and personal growth opportunities. I provide in this book specific examples of how the environment at Andesa was deliberately created, but in reality, the environment is as much the result of countless, sub-conscious actions and responses to situations. It is the soul of the individual at work, quietly, for the most part, guiding the firm in the direction of doing the right thing. To be truly effective, the beliefs of the individual, of all the individuals affecting the environment of a place, must be deep-seated and not for show.

Clearly, I believed CTA had value issues that were impacting personnel in negative ways. I had observed managers demanding results from their employees without giving them the tools, the incentive, or the proper mix of guidance and freedom to develop and succeed. They were failing to meet their obligations to the employees and placing the blame for the ensuing problems on those very same employees. Were the managers intentionally sabotaging their employees and thus the success of the firm? Of course not; they simply were not good managers. In an attempt to address this issue, I became increasingly vocal about protecting the people at CTA. At the time, I believe that CTA did not look for the potential value of the individual beyond what he or she could do for the company at that very moment. The company did not respect its employees enough to nurture and grow them because its primary focus was on the short-run measure of what the employee could do for CTA. The environment was unsupportive and insincere. It was clear that, as a result, the employees of CTA were not responding favorably to the company's needs.

While writing this book, I have wondered whether or not I am being too harsh in describing CTA. Many good people, including Mac, worked there. No doubt I am being harsh. But this book is not the place to gloss over shortcomings that negatively affect others. As much as possible, I want to shine a spotlight on bad situations that stemmed from an unhealthy environment, and then provide an alternative way of thinking.

I believe that this approach will build a better model of the firm.

Although my efforts to change the culture were just beginning, my focus on personnel was momentarily interrupted at the end of my first year at CTA when a crisis arose within the company. A disagreement between Hal Covert and an external partner ended in an agreement to dissolve the partnership. The external partner operated an administrative system that he had previously developed for CTA. Without him, a major part of the company's business would disappear. Hal asked me to construct an alternative system to be operated within the company. I told him that I knew nothing about developing a life insurance-driven benefits system, but that I would try. Knowing that the firm's days were numbered if we didn't replace the admin system quickly, I asked how long he thought it would take to build such a thing.

"It's exceedingly complex," Hal told me. "Probably about three years to get it up and running." CTA was in trouble. Judging by Hal's rough estimate, I could not complete the task in time to save the business. But I said again that I would try, and I dived into the unknown waters. I didn't know it then, but I was embarking on the creation of a solution that would lead to the formation of a new company.

To set the stage, I really did not like life insurance. I didn't like the way it was illustrated or the manner in which it was sold. I believed that, with my formal training in uncertainty and the time value of money, I understood well the concept of life insurance. Yet when a salesman tried to sell me a policy, it was as if nothing made sense. Few of the underlying concepts upon which the insurance was based were presented and related to my situation. Most of what I heard, I uncharitably considered sales fluff. Now, I asked myself, am I to take on the administration of the beast?

As I applied myself to the task of learning our system, my fears were confirmed. It was indeed an unruly beast. There was no written documentation explaining the system. When I asked the system users for an explanation of what it meant and how it was used, I was greeted with blank stares. I was told that the system was self explanatory. I am not a professional computer programmer. I have, however, written enough software programs to doubt that answers would be so easily forthcoming. I now understood why Hal thought we had a computer problem.

Here was a concrete example of personnel conflicts affecting the company's ability to function. In some ways it was the classic example of a breakdown in communication between the generalist and the specialist. CTA's generalists were its sales and counseling people. As a group, they simply did not know how to communicate with the benefits analysis group (the specialists). Nor did they accept the responsibility to learn how to articulate their needs to the analytical group in language that the analysts could understand. The problem was compounded by analysts who considered the sales / counseling staff incompetent. As a group, they were specialists with little respect for the unique skills necessary to succeed in sales and counseling. Neither side would move toward the other; obviously, they never met. At the time, I recognized this as a fundamental, deep-seated lack of respect—something anathema to a firm with a soul—but I did not know how to solve the problem. Later, it would be resolved in two ways. First, a section of the company would develop a healthy culture, thereby modeling what the environment should be; and second, changes in personnel would weed out the least cooperative employees.

In spite of the frustration of an unhealthy environment, I continued trying to learn the system. My next attempt was a request for the source code and any documentation from the external ex-partner. The source code arrived along with a note stating that no written documentation was available.

The nuances of the system were all in the head of the external partner, and he was not about to go through the laborious process of creating written documentation. That was not part of the separation agreement.

I then began to look at the code itself. Fortunately, it was written in the one programming language that I knew. I was looking for comment statements, which I quickly determined were non-existent. (For readers not familiar with computer code, comment statements, which are ignored by the computer, are placed in the code by the programmer as clues to the significance of certain operations. Generally speaking, the more comment statements, the better.) To compound matters, the variable names (such as insurance amount, premium amount, etc.) consisted of X's, Y's, and Z's rather than having descriptive names. I was depressed. How could I make sense of this mess? I felt like an amateur tracker asked to observe a maze of muddled prints in a snowy field and determine what creatures had made them, where they were going, and why.

Tempted as I was, quitting was not an option. I hadn't taken the job with the thought of giving up. And in the end, the wretched condition of the system turned out to be a blessing. Six months of intense digging and drudgery taught me more about the do's and don't's of this insurance/benefits system than I would have ever been patient enough to discover under more favorable conditions.

Two lessons proved vital to my development of a quality, workable alternative administration system. First, I learned that the basic framework of the current system was fundamentally flawed. The life insurance company ("carrier") whose insurance we used to provide the benefits had become most vexed with the information the old system provided. Clients, especially the flagship client Phillips Petroleum, would ask the carrier to explain certain results, and they could not. Numbers did not tally from year to year, and it was not always clear what they meant. Phillips was an important client for the carrier, so these shortcomings received high-level scrutiny. Second, as I gained overall knowledge of the system, I learned that, when properly constructed and utilized, this type of tax-advantaged financial vehicle had the potential to be highly effective. Even though I still faced a daunting task, I was heartened by the possibilities.

After six months of analyzing dead software, I convinced myself that I could take my new knowledge and build a superior system from scratch, complete with documentation and user involvement. But I was going to need considerable help. I had Mike, who was a competent, qualified assistant, but what I needed was a pro. I needed someone to build a solid framework, within which I could write the application specific code. My first thought was Dave March, the best software engineer I've ever met. I knew Dave from my days as director of the Lehigh Computing Center. When I told him what I needed, he was intrigued by the project and agreed to join as a consultant. We spent many a night defining the system, with Dave interrogating me as to what I wanted to build and why. If my answers were vague or did not ring true, he would hammer away until I understood what he needed and what I had to specify. Ours was a great partnership which was to last for many more years. It was also the beginning of a shift in the environment of CTA. Suddenly we had specialists cooperating with generalists, teaching each other how to communicate, making the extra effort to get the job done right.

Nine months after we began the project, Phillips Petroleum, our largest client, was up and running with a totally new set of comprehensive reports. I had been working twelve hours a day for more than a year, but, with a lot of help from Dave and Mike, the system was completed in half the time Hal Covert had estimated, yet barely in time to save CTA. It took another year to convert the remaining clients. An environment of cooperation, mutual respect, professional pride, and the honesty to admit and correct mistakes had been created in one segment of the company. This nucleus would grow until it became the soul of the firm rather than isolated positive relationships in a sea of indifference.

The new system not only worked, it worked well. The carrier checked for errors but found none. Phillips personnel finally understood the nuances of the benefit plan CTA had designed for them. And lastly, the carrier no longer received confused inquiries from Phillips that they were at a loss to answer. We finally had a product we could be proud of, one that came much closer to giving the client what they needed than had our original system. The goodwill so generated would prove invaluable in the future.

During this time, I was involved in the hiring of several new employees. At Lehigh I had participated in the hiring process on a regular basis. I had grown to appreciate the importance of hiring people who, by their very makeup, would make a positive contribution to the environment. As an economist, I knew that an individual's contribution was not only what she produced directly but also how she affected the production of other individuals. I tried to ask each prospective employee questions that would give me at least an inkling of who, deep down, she was. Now that I was at CTA, where I was trying to build a new atmosphere, I was especially concerned with bringing in people with good attitudes.

One day, Howard Snyder and I were interviewing an applicant for a financial analyst position, and I pointed out to the candidate that she seemed especially enthusiastic about the position. Then I said, "But I'm concerned that you don't know enough about it to be so enthusiastic." Financial and estate planning was Howard's area of the firm, and this was an excellent candidate. Howard started fidgeting, and I sensed his discomfort. (Later he told me that he thought my comment had cost us the candidate.) But quick as lightening, the young lady responded with maturity beyond her years. "I really know a great deal about you from the way you're conducting the interview," she said. "I have a bachelor's degree in mathematics. Every other company I've interviewed with has focused on how that will translate into specific duties. All they want to know is how I will benefit their company. You, on the other hand, are clearly interested in my overall attitude and fundamental capability. " We offered her the position on the spot. CTA gained a valued employee that day, but that wasn't all. From this unlikely feedback in the middle of an interview, we came to recognize that there was something special about the process we were using to screen prospective employees.

Shortly thereafter, I was interviewing a candidate for an administrative assistant position. What appeared to be a routine hiring event turned out to be a watershed moment for the firm. From the moment Linda Ellison (LE) walked into my office, she struck me as an exceptionally open person, one who was interested in communicating, not projecting an image. Her resume said she had been salutatorian of her high school class. She had scored especially high on the aptitude test she had taken earlier in the day. I knew she was smart and had the skills to do the job, but I wanted to know who she was. I wanted to understand her as a person. Eventually, I asked her the question I asked all prospects: *What makes you tick?* I wish I remembered now the answer she gave. I only remember that it was good, that it helped me decide that I wanted her to be part of the firm. But for LE, it wasn't about the answer. The question was what made up her mind. She was so taken by the question, so inspired by the idea that we would want to know her at that level, that she said to herself right then, "I don't know if they will offer me a job, but if they do I'll grab it. This is the kind of place I want to work."

I cannot recall the exact motivation for interviewing in this way. I certainly wanted to employ the best people possible and I searched for ways to engage them in the process of determining if they would serve the company well. But I'd like to believe that I truly cared for them as individuals and wanted to avoid placing people in jobs where they could not find fulfillment.

For the first year, LE did not work for me. It would be years, in fact, before she told me of her experience coming to CTA for the job interview, of the magic that occurred for her that day. But the process of hiring her reinforced ideas I had been formulating about finding good people and giving them the freedom to impart their talents and their values into the environment of the firm.

Throughout this period, CTA's financial stress affected everyone involved with the firm. The principals were drawing partial salary and accounts payable were stretched to the limit. Something had to give. Reducing staff was one of the options available to save the firm, but we struggled mightily over the idea of terminating staff due to problems not of their making. Honestly, it might have been easier to shut down the firm rather than make selective termination decisions. We finally concluded, however, that it would be cowardly not to try to salvage the firm, so we eliminated fourteen positions—nearly half the staff. Still we were operating in the red, but our chances at survival were greatly improved.

In deciding to fire employees in an attempt to save the firm, had we allowed the welfare of CTA alone to justify our treatment of the staff we let go? Had we allowed the end to justify the means? Some people thought so. In fact, one of the employees caught in the downsizing accused us of just that. But we had weighed the plight of each person involved, and since the options were to downsize or shut down the only variable was how many people would lose their jobs. We let go the people we felt were least likely to flourish at CTA, making them the people least likely to add value to the company and most likely to find greater fulfillment elsewhere. It was regrettable; it was painful; but it was the right thing to do.

The bare bones staff that now made up CTA was receptive to the notion that, in response to our financial troubles we had been running harder instead of smarter and that the attitude of the firm would have to shift if we were to survive. We all had sufficient experience to understand that running smarter did not mean simply changing the goal. It meant rethinking the means by which we reached our goals. CTA's senior management came to the conclusion that we would have to change our focus to the journey rather than simply hailing the destination. During the process of restructuring, we attempted to refocus by incorporating the components of an ethical environment into the daily operation of the firm. We promoted honest work, cooperation, and industriousness, without which the firm didn't have a chance. Some of the remaining staff knew we were on the right track, and they jumped on board. Others doubted, and they chose to leave what they considered a sinking ship. What we lost in capability when staff members left, we gained in steps toward a healthier, more cooperative environment.

One of the heroes of the company at that time was Harriet Redman. Along with myriad other tasks, Harriet answered the telephone. Increasingly, the calls were from suppliers wanting to know when they would be paid. How she did it I don't know, but Harriet was able to pacify the callers and always maintain a bright outlook. Her job had become exceedingly difficult, but she knew we were aware of her situation and were doing our best to improve it. She readily embraced her task, and her positive attitude was an example for all of us and contributed greatly to the establishment of a healthy environment. Our financial stress was not relieved until 1986, but that story is told in the next chapter.

During a senior management meeting in the summer of 1982, Mac Briggs turned to me and said, "John, you look tired. Do you need more help? We could bring in another technical assistant." This offer to hire an additional employee may sound odd when we had just eliminated fourteen positions, but we desperately needed resources if we were to pursue the areas that held promise for the survival of the company.

"I do need help," I admitted, "but not technical help. What I need is an organized, intelligent, and conscientious assistant. Someone like Linda Ellison." LE, at that time, was assisting three of our benefit plan counselors.

Mac responded, "Why someone *like* Linda? Why not Linda herself?" I pointed out that replacing LE would cause the counselors for whom she was working real adjustment pains. Someone else pointed out that replacing her in that position would be far easier than finding the proper person for me. So it came to be that LE joined the part of the company that would later become Andesa, and her presence there immediately began defining the firm's culture. When LE accepted an assignment, I could forget it; it was done properly in both spirit and letter. She was impeccably honest. She was enthusiastic. Her work ethic was beyond reproach, and fortunately she thrived on challenging assignments. I had developed an appreciation for LE as a person through our lengthy interview process.

Even before we started working directly together, I knew that she would relieve my workload, but more importantly I believed that together we could take major steps toward building the kind of firm we both yearned for. LE became a soul mate. She was a person who valued, above all else, the type of environment I was trying to foster at CTA. Her presence within the firm quickly added strength and conviction to my goal of building an employee-centric environment. The progression from one to two was a critical jump. The culture shift generated by the opportunity to discuss with a like-minded person the little ethical issues encountered daily cannot be overestimated.

The first new client to test our rebuilt administrative capabilities was a major West Coast corporate prospect, The Signal Companies, Inc. We were convinced that with our new system we could provide them with an executive benefit plan significantly superior to the one they were currently using, and we told them so. But month after month we tried to meet their needs with off-the-shelf life insurance products without success. We were not prepared for the possibility that we had miscalculated the feasibility of the job. The situation was made worse by the fact that, based on our prior experience, we had advised Dick Cotton (a CTA partner) that we would be successful, and Dick had staked his reputation on his promise to Signal's CFO that we would deliver a superior solution.

One night, in the thick of our failure with Signal, I began having chest pains that I feared were a heart attack. It turned out that I was fine—a bad case of indigestion—but the realization that I could let the situation create this much stress was sobering. The next day I met with Mac and we vowed that we would not allow a repeat of this experience. In this case, we had allowed an end—the acquisition of Signal as a client—to justify means, promising something we were not at all certain we could deliver. In spite of our exhausting efforts to live up to our misguided promise, a successful outcome of the Signal project seemed unlikely.

Had we been alone in this venture, we might well have accepted defeat. We had a highly exposed partner, however, so giving up was not an option easily accepted. We persevered not because we had carefully analyzed the potential for success and found the odds to our liking, but because we owed it to everyone involved to try to come up with a viable solution. But we understood now that it was time to restart with a healthy, honest approach. We admitted that, no matter how hard we pushed ourselves, we couldn't do the job with the tools we had. So we decided to build new tools. We set out to design the functional characteristics of a life insurance policy we believed could handle this segment of the market. When complete, we used computer simulation to test its performance relative to the best existing products. Tests revealed that our policy would be significantly superior to available products.

The million dollar question now was: What do we do with this knowledge, with respect to Signal? Dick and I knew that, come what may, we could not continue to make unsubstantiated promises. We decided, with great trepidation on Dick's part, to present a solution based on our theoretical insurance product and identify it as just that: theoretical. Dick rightly feared that Signal's CFO would throw us out of his office when he heard the word theoretical. But to our relief and surprise, the CFO was intrigued by our solution. He asked how long it would take to deliver a service based on our design. When I estimated that we could have it up and running in nine months, he told us that, if we could indeed deliver within this time frame, they would purchase our service.

The insurance company that we were working with was willing to manufacture a new life insurance policy based on our design, but their willingness came with one major condition: we would have to provide the policy administration service normally provided by their own back office. They were not readily able to do so, in this case, due to the unorthodox nature of the design. We had no such administrative experience, but after discussing the respective responsibilities, we agreed that we could and would administer the policy. The insurance company's willingness to let us administer one of their products, something they had never done before, resulted from the faith their Executive Vice President had in our firm, trust that he based on our performance in the Phillips case and others.

Although we now had to build a new, complex system in a short amount of time, I was delighted. We had been upfront with Signal about our failure, our capabilities, and the theoretical nature of our eventual solution, and they had responded positively. Through honesty and hard work, we had put ourselves in the position of creating a new product that would give us a competitive advantage in the marketplace, by providing a service built from the ground up to address the needs of our market. Administering the product would provide us with the control necessary to make a major improvement in the services provided to clients. Again, we brought in Dave March as the overall system architect.

With the new life insurance policy, we were successful in delivering the performance we had projected, and Signal became a client in September 1983. Although the contract was of modest size, this client and our relationship with them was a benchmark for our firm. To meet their need, we were required to become insurance policy administrators, a service that is an important core of our operations today. And more importantly, we were emphasizing a policy of open, honest communication between our employees and clients. Accordingly, we cite this date as the birth of Andesa. While the company had yet to acquire the name Andesa, it had, without a doubt, developed the employee-centric mindset and the basic functional capability that are the soul of this firm.

*Chapter Seven*

# Formalizing the Culture, 1983–2002

"Andesa" is one of those names that beg to be explained. In fact, people involved with the company are asked routinely about it origins. The name was the result of a brainstorming session Mac Briggs and I had in 1985. We were still Covert and Associates back then, but Hal Covert had just left the firm and we wanted to change the name. We wanted a short, unique name that would not require revision each time the nature of the business changed. So we played around with a lot of ideas, and at some point we tried combining the last two letters of the eldest child of the three principal owners. Mac's daughter Evan gave us the "An," my son Wade, the "de," and Bob Rust's daughter Lisa, the "sa." Andesa. By design, it has no intrinsic meaning, and we thought it had a nice ring to it.

Although it wasn't officially named Andesa Services, Inc. until 2004, we measure the firm's existence from September 1983, the date when the unique essence that is Andesa first coalesced. At this critical point in time, Andesa had established: (1) a strong, employee-centric culture; (2) personnel with commitment to service and excellence; (3) a compelling vision for a unique service; and (4) the software and technical knowhow to compete in the highly specialized corporate-owned, life insurance (COLI) market.[1] At this point, Andesa was acting as both a broker and an administrator for a single carrier in the COLI market. Over the next twenty years, Andesa would learn, by trial and error, how to incorporate this essence into a culture that is healthy for its employees, and thus for its clients and shareholders as well.

In retrospect, we must have seemed the most arrogant entity in our marketplace. We were a fraction of the size of our competitors. In fact, we were but a blip on their radar, but we had an advantage that we believed would soon shake up the market. We, at that time, meant LE, Terrill Frantz, and me. Terrill had replaced Mike two years before, when Mike left to join his father in business. But it was LE's presence in the firm that lit things on fire as far as the firm's culture was concerned. She and I shared a vision for the firm, and together we could sense the opportunity that lay before us: opportunity to make great things happen in our industry, but also opportunity to do it the right way. The environment had evolved ethically to one

The picture on the right is a recent one of Linda Ellison, who remains with Andesa as a member of its senior management team.

---

[1] The COLI market is essentially where insurance companies (carriers), brokers (independent agents of the carriers), and corporations work together to develop and administer financial benefits plans for executives.

that would support moral decision-making, no matter the cost. We had nurtured the environment because we believed in it, but at the same time we hoped that the positive culture would translate into positive performance in the marketplace.

With LE on board, we quickly learned that each had the other's best interests at heart. This freed us to speak our minds, knowing that our remarks would be interpreted as positively as they were intended. Neither of us was satisfied with providing an adequate insurance product. We wanted excellence. In addition, we were energized by the prospect that our administrative support of this product would be outstanding. We were free to aim high because, in an open, honest environment, there was no shame in errors or failures that stemmed from hard work and valiant efforts. Combined with a sense of fair play, honesty, and trust, it is amazing how industriousness can cause productivity to soar.

Along with the environment and the personnel, early Andesa was shaped by its compelling vision. I call Andesa's vision compelling because we were not simply responding to what our clients required. We were, after considerable thought, responding to their unspoken needs. In a sense, we were following the Golden Rule. We knew the market, we had experience there, and we had made a conscious decision to provide nothing less for our clients than what we would have wanted for ourselves. For example, it was standard at the time for insurance companies to generate life insurance policy results annually, thus limiting reporting to a similar time frame. We didn't think that was good enough, so we designed our policy to operate on a monthly cycle and provided clients with updates twelve times a year. In addition, we alone readily had the ability to meet client needs for summary reports for any contiguous number of months for whatever purpose they required.

Our commitment to our dream was sorely tested as we got down to the business of running a successful, ethical firm. If, in the beginning, we did not have two nickels to rub together, now we did not have pennies. Moreover, our "compelling" vision was being questioned by the marketplace. We had challenged ourselves to be innovative, yet in doing so we scared away potential clients with the novelty of our ideas. We structured an insurance policy to be more effective for its specialized application. In fact, we provided services that some thought would never be necessary. In building our service, we followed three tenets. First, honesty demanded that we not do a superficial job. Second, clients did not always fully understand their needs. Just as Dave March had taken it upon himself to show me what was needed when we were working together to build our new system, Andesa saw it as an important aspect of our job to help clients think through their needs. And third, we refused to blindly accept clients' stated needs, for if we did we would forever be condemned to solving the same problem over and over. We would merely be solving manifestations of the real need.

We were the only firm in the industry that administered benefit plans and also did all of the detailed calculations of the insurance policies backing up these plans. The unprecedented access we had to detailed insurance information made all of this mechanically possible, but unfortunately it did not initially convince clients that it was something they needed. We had created a powerful tool that allowed us to provide our clients with extensive reporting that answered essentially every conceivable question. The only question we couldn't answer, it seemed, was: Why on Earth would I need to know all that?

What we possessed in technical and data management skills, we lacked initially in sales skills. Selling this better mousetrap proved more difficult than expected. Time and again, perspective clients balked at the idea of converting to a service that could solve problems they hadn't yet encountered. Business got so bad that, in August of 1985, I requested that the Board of Directors of The Andesa Companies consider whether we should continue or if our efforts in the life insurance arena should be abandoned and the staff reassigned to other activities. At the time, the principals were drawing bare minimal compensation. We were so thinly capitalized as to be operating with the aid of a bank loan which required not only the principals but also their spouses to back up the loan with a pledge of all personal assets. In spite of the risk, I believed we should continue, but I felt it was inappropriate for us to do so, given the situation, without an explicit go-ahead from the board. Of the four board members, one voted to abandon the endeavor, Mac and I voted to stay the course, and one abstained from voting. By the slightest margin, Andesa was given a reprieve.

The board's decision to continue was incredibly fortunate. Over the next five months, the marketplace caught up with what we had to offer. Our innovative policy design was finally accepted by independent actuaries. Prospects began to understand the value behind a tool that allowed them to quickly obtain answers to unforeseen questions. Because we had organized the reports in layers such that the client need go only to the depth they required at the time, the product was user-friendly and flexible. Business poured in at such a pace that we were suddenly stretched to our limits, both physically and mentally. The affirmation that we were headed in the right direction was enough to make the challenge of absorbing the new business a labor of love. By early 1986, the profit from our activity (about twenty percent of the parent company) had returned the parent company to solid profitability and begun eliminating accrued debt. It was an exhilarating period for LE, Terrill, and me. Today, through the miracle of online databases and powerful query software, Andesa's approach to providing policy information has been expanded by more than tenfold.

During this period of rapid growth, we were careful not to hire anyone prematurely. Finances were certainly a factor in our caution, but more importantly we felt a deep concern for the serious obligation we as a firm would have to anyone we hired. We had been required to let good people go during the restructuring of CTA, and we were committed to avoiding another planning failure. In fact, from 1983 through the present, we have never terminated an employee solely for financial reasons. Eventually, however, the onslaught of demand became too much for LE and me to handle, so in 1986 we decided to add a second senior employee to the staff. We felt keenly the need to bring the right kind of person on board. The approach for this hire, we decided, would be even more deliberate than when we hired LE. We recognized that selection of employees was absolutely critical if we were to maintain and enhance the environment that we had worked so hard to create. We also expected that continued growth would require a more systematic approach to hiring, one that reflected our conviction that we should be forthright and explain fully the position, the environment, and the selection process *before* we even asked an applicant to apply.

The approach we settled on went something like this. First, we placed an ad in the local newspaper stating the available position and directing individuals interested in more information to simply supply us with a mailing address. Upon receipt of a query, we mailed a packet of information, including a detailed description of the Andesa culture, by return mail. If the applicant subsequently applied, we acknowledged receipt of the application by return mail and set a reply date. Within the specified timeframe, we mailed the applicant either regrets or a request to schedule an interview. During the interview process, we disclosed how many candidates would be interviewed and we provided the candidate ample time to ask additional questions. Finally, we made an offer to our preferred candidate within three days of the last interview and sent regrets to any candidate not deemed appropriate.

Serious candidates responded favorably to this approach and told us so routinely. One item in the packet we sent to prospective applicants was a request for a statement explaining why they were interested in a position with our firm. The question was designed to screen out applicants who seemed to be simply seeking a job. While acquiring a job is a worthy goal, we were looking for stronger motivation than that. The statements of interest provided us with much more useful information than we had anticipated. Many applicants commented on the process itself. They were taken by our willingness to tell them about the company before we asked about them. Apparently, this is highly unusual. They appreciated the seriousness we conveyed by the completeness of the process. They appreciated our efforts to keep them apprised of their progress. Virtually all who were interviewed stated that their interest in the firm was favorably influenced by our hiring process.

Providing prospects with detailed information about Andesa had the unanticipated benefit of putting them in the position to actively participate in the interview process. This turned out to be a key to hiring people with values and initiative. We learned a great deal more about people when they knew a lot about us. It was easy to spot candidates who had taken the time to read about the company. They had comments and serious questions about our goals, our mission, and the Andesa culture. Our philosophy was that prospects who lacked initiative and values compatible with Andesa's likely would become problems. Core values do not change readily. With their active participation, the hiring process lost some of the uncertainty that we found unacceptable.

We implemented our new hiring philosophy for the first time in 1986 when we hired Kim Bohling, a talented, analytical individual who fit our standard profile. Through this process, we found that Kim was qualified skills-wise, but we also learned that she was impeccably honest, interested in doing meaningful work, and intelligent. It was the combination of her skills and her character that made her the right kind of person for Andesa. As it turned out, Kim's greatest contribution to Andesa was that she was an excellent team member. Her values proved to be every bit as important to the firm as was her analytical skill. Kim stayed with the firm, reinforcing the ethical environment, until she and her husband relocated to Washington where he had taken a new job.

I have explained our employee selection process in such detail because every environment works best when its people share its core values, goals, and beliefs, and Andesa is no exception. Thus, it is crucial to carefully select people who will be good fits. It is important both for the benefit of the prospective employee and for the benefit of the company. The environment we provide, while nurturing, has the added characteristic that it requires that we employ people who want to be nurtured toward bettering themselves, people who have a measure of drive and self initiative. Individuals lacking these attributes tend to flounder in the freedom of a trusting environment in which managers understand that close guidance can stifle creativity and personal growth. I am continually amazed by the sheer number of exceptional people Andesa hires, people who feel they have never had the opportunity to

The picture on the right is a recent one of Bill Smith, who remains with Andesa as a member of its senior management team.

pursue success. We have benefited greatly as a company and as human beings from the quality people we have been able to hire based in part on our hiring practice.

In 1987, we hired our fourth key employee. Our goal was to replace Terrill, who had recently left the firm, with someone who had the potential to handle our growing need for technical knowhow. Instead of continuing to purchase computing time, as we had since 1979, we had acquired our own small computer in 1985. The operating system was UNIX, whose user interface, at the time, was primitive by any standard. While it provided an improvement over our previous computing environment, the system required a dedicated and capable operator, someone with a unique understanding of a state-of-the-art computer system. Due to the nature of the job, the number of qualified prospects was small. It quickly became obvious that we would have to compromise our profile; we weren't going to find the kind of person we were looking for with the skills we needed.

Our search had come down to two finalists, each representing a different compromise. One had the skills to provide immediate support of our requirements. The other had a great attitude and apparent value system as well as strong fundamental skills, but he lacked the specific skills to immediately meet our needs. Kim, LE, and I met to make a decision. Before any discussion, I decided to take a straw vote to see where we stood. The vote was two to one in favor of hiring the candidate who could immediately handle the new system but whose overall attitude and values were less to our liking. We were all people who prized values, yet the pressure to achieve the "end" of immediate relief tempted us to accept inappropriate means. Before the official vote, the discussion shifted to one of values and the Andesa culture, and when it was time to cast our votes, we unanimously chose the second individual: Bill Smith. Although we expected it to take Bill six months to reach the level of expertise required to run UNIX, we made a calculated decision to care for Andesa's long-term health. My father, I believe, would think we got it right.

The hiring of Bill Smith was a key test of our commitment to an employee-centric environment. We knew that the Andesa culture required individuals who would support and maintain it, but were we willing to pay the *very* high price of delay in order to have a person join us who would enhance the already excellent working relationships within our unit? Under great stress, we chose not to allow the desire for immediate relief to justify a short-term solution that threatened the environment. This was an important milestone in formalizing our desire to build a firm with a soul. How a perspective employee will fit with the Andesa culture shifted, at this point, from an afterthought to a primary consideration. Bill Smith is still with the firm in a leadership technical position. He believes that the environment in which he works has benefited him as a whole person. We believe, likewise, that his intelligence, character, and attitude have made up for any delays the company may have endured while he got up to speed on UNIX. Today, Bill knows more about the needs of our clients and the technology employed to meet those needs than anyone else at Andesa.

By January 1987, I had totally removed myself from the sale of life insurance and transferred that part (insurance brokerage) of our business to Mac Briggs. My staff and I focused exclusively on insurance policy administration and limited benefits plan administration. Removing ourselves from brokerage operations eliminated a conflict of interest. As a life insurance administrator, I had access to information that could improve my performance at the expense of other salesmen whose policies we administered. It did not matter that I avoided accessing such information. The potential was there, and it caused concern. As our administrative activity increased we wanted to make this separation of activities very clear, so on January 1, 1989, we incorporated as an autonomous company and called ourselves Andesa TPA, Inc.[2]

Shortly after becoming Andesa TPA, we faced an interesting pricing situation for ongoing services with a prospective client. Our basic model is to bill monthly, and the billing consists of a base charge plus a charge that varies with volume. The base charge recovers our fixed costs, and the per capita charge recovers our incremental costs. Each includes a profit component. Our fixed costs are relatively high due to the substantial investment we have made in systems development and staff training. One day, a prospective client explained that his superiors viewed everything in terms of average cost, which, due to our pricing, would be unacceptably high during the first few years as his volume built. He requested that we consider an alternative pricing schedule to address his situation. We reviewed his business model carefully and decided to prepare the special schedule for him. We lowered the base pricing significantly, increased the incremental pricing significantly, and factored in a consideration for the risk we were taking. Our goal was to recover, on a present value basis, lost initial revenue over time.

After a number of years, this client's volume had increased such that current profits were recovering lost initial profits by a significant margin. While his activity indicated that this would continue indefinitely, he had no complaints with the pricing schedule in effect. I met with him shortly after this shift in volume and explained that on a cumulative basis we had been made whole. Then I told him that, effective the following month, we would switch him back to our normal pricing schedule. This change meant a decrease in his total billing, a savings that would grow even more if his volume increased. We

---

[2] TPA stands for third party administrator, which reasonably describes what we did. We were an independent entity that provided services to insurance companies and the brokers who sold their life insurance policies.

had no obligation to make this adjustment, nor did he expect or ask us to do so. He had been in a difficult spot years earlier, and we had helped him out. We had been compensated for the risk, and we believed that squeezing additional profits forever was simply not ethical. Obtaining additional profits to pay for the risk we took was good business; taking advantage of his difficult situation to obtain profits beyond that was not. The client was both surprised and eternally grateful. For many years, until he sold his company and retired, he was an enthusiastic client and sang our praises at industry meetings. We don't face such situations every day, but we do face smaller ones periodically, and we try to respond comparably. We try to avoid the bureaucratic approach of mechanically responding to situations, because an automatic, policy-dictated response, while it might allow us to avoid difficult decisions and eliminate judgment calls, would de-humanize the client, and ultimately it would fail both the client and ourselves. So, one aspect of formalizing our culture meant, in essence, consciously avoiding formalizing our relationships with our individual clients.

In January 1990, I accepted a position as CEO of a national specialty brokerage firm headquartered in Dallas, Texas. At the same time I maintained my position as CEO of Andesa. Although the time frame was not specified, it was understood that I would hold the new position for no more than five years. I had a specific job to do for the Dallas firm, and they, in return, offered interesting and potential benefits for Andesa. They, for instance, were strong in marketing, the area that was our greatest weakness. In spite of the potential benefits, my move to Dallas challenged Andesa. My absence meant that Andesa's staff would have to assume additional responsibilities. They proved more than willing to do whatever they could to make it happen. Apart from the anticipated benefits from this relationship, an unforeseen opportunity arose. My personal exposure to insurance companies as CEO of the Dallas firm created expanding opportunities for Andesa to work with new insurance companies.

In January 1993, I returned to Andesa full-time. Six months later, in the summer of 1993, I met with Andesa's senior staff and told them that I was retiring. I wanted to slow down and sample retired life. This was not ill-considered on my part, but it was incredibly difficult. I had invested a great deal of myself in Andesa over the previous sixteen years, but my absence of three years suggested that the company would do fine without my operational management. I had built close relationships with many people at Andesa over the years, and the thought of these fading was most unpleasant. On the other side, my three-year tenure at the Dallas firm had exhausted me, and I believed new management blood was needed. The people of Andesa voiced their concern that another John Walker could not be found. I agreed, but quickly went on to point out that another John Walker was not what Andesa needed; a new set of skills was now in order. It was time for us to move from a successful entrepreneurial firm to a successfully managed firm.

As it turned out, Andesa's employees were right to be concerned. The transition we were facing is one of the most difficult in business, and the failure rate is high. Indeed, the transition went poorly. Although we followed our careful hiring procedure, the first CEO we hired did not work out. Immediately after he began running the company, I watched him respond to a situation in what I can only describe as a self-centered way. As time passed, I saw more questionable behavior and a clear disinclination to collaborate. After the first year, I was ready to terminate him, but the staff wanted to give him more time to prove himself. After the second year, I had seen no improvement, and I detected concern among the staff as well. I made the difficult decision at this point to terminate Andesa's CEO. When I met with the staff to announce the firing, they unanimously agreed with my action.

They also strongly requested that I not be in a hurry to find another replacement. I returned to the firm in a reduced role.

I stayed on as CEO this time for several years, but the time for me to retire had in fact come and gone. I was newly married to my wife, Diane, and living part of the year in Florida. While Diane has been very supportive of my business interests, during this time she could not help but occasionally ask, "Just what is it that makes you think you're retired?"

When I began considering another attempt to find the right fit for Andesa's CEO, I realized that we needed a better hiring process for this position. The one that had served us so well in the past had failed us when applied to a very senior management position. We had learned a lot through our first attempt to find a new CEO, and one of the lessons was that we needed help with the process. Accordingly, we retained the services of an executive recruiting firm. We knew we were on the right track when Jerry Weiss, a partner in the recruiting firm, asked to visit Andesa for two days so he could better understand its culture. Jerry also explained that if we wanted a good leader, we would have to go out and find one; good candidates typically were not reading the want ads. This time we settled on an enthusiastic entrepreneur. I felt good about the choice and the process we had used to make it, but after only a month our new CEO resigned. He was gracious and apologetic in his explanation that the culture at Andesa was not for him and the travel impact on his family was more negative than he anticipated. I appreciated his candor and ability to arrive at a quick decision. Once again I resumed my duties as CEO, this time with a sinking feeling that I might never be able to pull off Andesa's transition to a successfully managed firm.

During this period of growth and restructuring, Andesa's staff became increasingly concerned about the impact of change on our firm's culture and outlook. It took some time to realize that the culture that had made our firm successful could not be taken for granted. We were still a small company, about sixteen employees, but the culture was well understood and tested. It was also, as we had begun to understand, dependent on its people and subject to influence by changes in personnel. Accordingly, in April 1997, we took a further step toward formalizing our culture by creating a document that spelled out our vision, our mission, and our values. In February 2002 the document was slightly modified to read, as it does today, that the vision of the firm is to "provide an environment that encourages and facilitates employees to develop and apply their business skills to the fullest in order to benefit the employee, the client, and the shareholder."

In late 1998, a development in our sister company, The Andesa Companies, began a process that would radically change the face of Andesa. Mac Briggs and two fellow COLI brokers had lost faith in the large administrative firm from whom they received support vital to their business. Rather than compromise their ethical standards in order to continue doing business with the organization, they decided to discontinue the relationship. Mac asked for my assistance in identifying an alternative source of support. We concluded that Mac and his friends should search for another service provider with compatible ethics. If that failed, but *only* if that failed, I recommended they undertake the difficult task of building their own company. A couple of months later, Mac informed me that they could not find a suitable provider. I had serious reservations about their abilities to operate an administration operation, and I told them so. All three were superb salesmen, but administrative support is an entirely different animal. "Hire someone," I advised Mac, "with strong personal values and solid support experience to build the company for you." And as I was speaking, it occurred to me that I knew just the person to run their administrative services.

I had met Vince Collier six months before, while interviewing him for the position of COO of Andesa. I actually offered him the job, which he ultimately declined because he and his family found themselves unwilling to relocate from Sarasota to Allentown. But there was no reason he would have to move to build a new company. Since Vince had already gone through the lengthy interview process for Andesa, Mac and his friends felt comfortable extending an offer with little additional scrutiny. Vince accepted the position of President and CEO of ADASTAR and assembled an excellent staff. ADASTAR would provide support services to Mac and his colleagues. Because Andesa provided related services to a large number of brokers, we recognized that, if I were in an ownership or management position with ADASTAR, there would be a conflict of interest. Accordingly, I did not become a shareholder in the new company, but Vince and I worked closely together as he built and operated the company.

ADASTAR was built on the concept that it would receive insurance policy data through an electronic link from Andesa. This dictated that ADASTAR would be limited to Andesa's carriers and associated life insurance products. This constraint limited Mac's and his partners' sales flexibility, but it also allowed ADASTAR to focus its attention and build its own staff to perform functions that were complimentary, not duplicative, of Andesa's operations.

In the fall of 2000, Vince Collier and I met with a representative of AEGON, one of Andesa's largest clients, to discuss their need for a tool that would effectively show prospective and actual policy holders what life insurance policies could reasonably be expected to do financially over a future span of time. We refer to such a tool as an illustration system. ADASTAR was in the process of developing a new, Internet-based illustration system that would tightly link with the Andesa policy administrative system. During the two-day meeting we all came to agree that AEGON would benefit from an alternative to the very expensive service they were using. We had nothing operational to offer at that time, but they liked the

ADASTAR concept we presented.

Clients, competitors, and independent actuaries had told us that an integrated system incorporating policy administration, policy illustration, and plan administration would not work, and that is exactly what ADASTAR and Andesa teamed up to accomplish. The reason for the skepticism was simple—an integrated system would be too cumbersome. The appeal of an integrated system, however, was that separate systems could not be perfectly synchronized. This inability to synchronize the systems led to misunderstandings and errors in calculations. Historically, the industry had put up with these flaws because there wasn't an identifiably better approach to the problem. While minor, these problems led to a lack of confidence, which everyone agreed was a significant issue. We realized that implementing an integrated system would be challenging, but we believed the increased accuracy and the added confidence it would instill in our clients would be worth the effort.

As was the case with The Signal Companies, AEGON decided they were willing to wait for the superior solution promised by ADASTAR. Soon after our meeting, they agreed to become the initial adopter of the illustration service. They were willing to go out on a limb to work with us based on two considerations. First, they recognized the power behind the unique capabilities offered by the Andesa/ADASTAR alliance, and second, they believed in Andesa. They had confidence in our integrity based on their experience working with us. AEGON was rewarded in the long run with expanded capabilities and savings of hundreds of thousands of dollars per year.

Over the next several years, Andesa continued to grow, but alas we had not solved the management succession problem. I was CEO still, although I was off-site and part-time, and I was in less of a hurry to find a replacement. Andesa was now stable and profitable. Perhaps we all suffered from the let-sleeping-dogs-lie affliction, but whatever the cause, we failed to foresee the drastic change that lay in the future. Chapter Eight presents the final awkward steps of a rocky transition and how our culture rose to the occasion to save the company from management missteps.

*Chapter Eight*

# Trial by Fire, 2003–2011

In the summer of 2003, ADASTAR merged with Andesa as a major division of Andesa. The boards of both companies had decided that they were already so tightly connected that there really was no downside to making the partnership official. Several of our clients had even made that suggestion. Merger, however, is like hiring: a good team fit is vital to the continued health of the organization. Like Andesa, ADASTAR was deeply committed to maintaining an employee-centric, ethical environment. Without the solid partnership between Andesa and ADASTAR, a partnership grounded in the shared values of the two organizations, successful merger would have been impossible.

So the two companies merged and continued working together to integrate policy administration, policy illustration, and plan administration into a single system. The resulting integrated solution has been a spectacular success, and Andesa's offerings have been served well by the system's enhanced capabilities. An unexpected benefit has been the ability of the illustration system to detect subtle errors in the policy administration system. Gradually, carriers have come to consider an integrated solution to be the best practice for the industry.

If we look at the process Andesa and its Distribution Services Division (formerly ADASTAR) went through in building our integrated solution, it is clear that the ethical environments enjoyed by both groups were instrumental in ensuring the success of the project. Because they felt free to speak their minds, employees from both firms made suggestions and voiced concerns. Because they were invested in the success of the company, they readily took on new challenges when obstacles presented themselves. With a change so revolutionary and a payoff so uncertain, the project never would have passed the most cursory review had earning a quick dollar been Andesa's aim. The concept of an integrated system was considered only because it was formulated in an environment that refused to judge it strictly as a return on investment.

While the culture at Andesa made the integrated solution possible, it did not make it easy. The marketplace was accustomed to the calculation of a particular illustration taking a few seconds, while our system took ten times that long. It didn't matter that the new system typically took far fewer iterations to create the desired solution. It didn't matter that the solution was more precise and conveyed information not otherwise available. Initially, users of the system were appalled by its slowness. A great deal of explanation, increased computing power, and software changes were required over several years to reduce this time differential to an acceptable level.

We were still working on the details of the integration project in 2004 when Andesa added a major new client. It took the better part of a year to work out the contracting details, at which point we should have known we were in over our heads. We were aware of two more potential clients, and we were eager to put our new system to work. There were plenty of signs warning us to slow down and regroup, but something fundamental had gone wrong. While the company's culture was solid, it was not perfect. At the same time that it was facilitating enthusiasm and honest good work among the junior employees, the environment had clearly broken down at the senior management level. Consisting of me (an off-site, part-time CEO) and two others, Andesa's leadership was communicating and cooperating at an all-time low.

The board, meanwhile, was mesmerized by the projected financial results of our growth and failed to ask the tough questions. We did not stop to ask: What will these new ventures do to our employee-centric environment? How will we manage an unprecedented rate of growth? At the November board meeting we passed a budget that incorporated a variable amount of new personnel resources that was dependent on how the new business played out. We all but ignored the growing issue of an increasingly inadequate infrastructure. The only significant effort we made to bolster our management was hiring Heather Horvath as Human Resources Manager. We knew Heather through her previous job and knew that she understood and believed in Andesa's environment. While her joining the firm helped alleviate some of Andesa's hiring issues, we were still woefully lacking in project, financial, and technical management.

By the fall 2005 board meeting, two things had become obvious. First, we needed a full-time CEO. I advised the board that I was retiring, and after a lengthy discussion we agreed to promote the COO to the position. I stepped down as CEO effective January 1, 2006. Second, the decision to pursue new market opportunities without the necessary breadth and depth of management resources was a disaster. Considering the challenging course we had set for ourselves, we were dangerously weak at the senior management level. At the same board meeting, we agreed to add three new management positions. This was a huge shift in Andesa that should have begun thirteen years prior, when we first attempted to move the company from an entrepreneurial firm to a managed one.

At this time, I reiterate the importance of hiring the right personnel. The personnel changes we were getting ready to make within Andesa would test our culture's ability to withstand growth. Would new blood alleviate our growing pains or alter our vision and challenge our environment? We had made hiring mistakes, but we also had acquired more than our share of exceptional individuals. The hiring process we had developed early on had served us well for ten years, but it was clear that we had outgrown it. We had supplemented it with the assistance of Jerry Weiss and his recruiting company and were ready to turn the entire task over to him. We abandoned the process, but held firm the philosophy of hiring good, ethical people. We knew that Jerry knew how to recruit at the senior management level. It was a difficult transition for us, but because Jerry had invested the time and energy into understanding Andesa's culture, we knew that he could recruit people who shared our philosophy.

As we expanded Jerry's role at Andesa, our executive search activity improved by an order of magnitude. Jerry placed Ron Scheese, our Chief Financial Officer and Chief Administrative Officer, and Rick Kendall, our Chief Technology Officer. Heather, through a local search, found Patty Zubia, who became Andesa's Director of Project Management. With the team of Jerry Weiss and Heather Horvath, we finally had the professional expertise necessary to locate and acquire the right senior personnel.

The events of the previous year and their effect on personnel were clearly evidenced in the countenance of Keith Hurst, whom I make an effort to talk with each time I visit Andesa. Keith is a senior developer and actuary who joined the company in May 1997. He is also a model for the expression: *What you see is what you get.* So, when I saw him in August 2005

I was concerned, and I immediately questioned him about his bedraggled appearance. He told me that he was working too hard, but more importantly, he didn't believe that his work was being well managed. He admitted that he was considering leaving the firm.

Three months later, after some of the new senior management had had time to settle in, I was back in Allentown for a board meeting, and I stuck my head into Keith's office to see how he was doing. By the look of him, things were improving. "You look like your spirits are up," I said. "Has your workload gotten more manageable?"

"Actually, John, I'm working more hours," he said. "But Rick Kendall has turned things around here. I feel like the work I'm doing will contribute to the company." I was glad to hear that Rick was making some positive changes.

In spite of our successful hires, it didn't take long to realize that we had yet to find the right CEO for Andesa. While surely a disappointment, this realization was not a surprise. Prior to formally offering our COO the job of CEO, I had told him that the board and I had reservations about his ability to do the job. He had been a good COO, and he wanted the job in spite of our reservations, so we offered him the opportunity to try. The warning signs began with the first financial reports, and, in spite of assurances that the financial picture would soon turn around, each successive set of reports was worse.

The external board members met alone in September to discuss the financial crisis and agreed to allow two more months before taking action. We had worked hard to repair the breakdown in senior management communication that had developed while I was still CEO, but by the fall 2006 board meeting, it was clear that communication between the board and senior management was deteriorating rapidly. The financial situation was continuing to deteriorate, yet it was increasingly difficult to get a straight assessment of where the company stood. Open and honest communication at all levels was an important component of Andesa's culture. It was something the firm had relied on from its conception to keep it on its moral course, something it had lost and paid the price for losing. And again, that communication was broken. Important things were not being said; concerns were being swept under the carpet. In addition, the CEO had pursued a failed strategy to shore up a need for technical resources. In desperation, albeit with the board's approval, he had aggressively acquired off-shore resources that proved to be ineffective and prohibitively expensive.

At the fall board meeting, we decided to terminate the CEO. Once again, I took on the duty of notifying the CEO of the board's decision, and once again I assumed the CEO title as we searched for a suitable permanent replacement.

Looking back on this period, it is easy to see that the transition from an entrepreneurial firm to a managed one was far more difficult than we had anticipated, in spite of all the literature that warns of this difficulty. For far too long, we failed to recognize the need for additional senior management. With appropriate management in place, we could have minimized bad business decisions. We never should have been in the position where we would appoint a questionable CEO. Our succession planning was reactive and undeveloped. Our failure to address the transition more effectively proved exceedingly costly in terms of employee morale, service to clients, and profitability. The fact that we operated in an ethical, employee-centric environment ultimately rescued us from ourselves, but it did not protect us initially from poor decision-making at the board level.

As a result of this series of poor decisions, we were, for the first time in ten years, under financial strain. The uncontrolled growth and subsequent acquisition of off-shore resources in an attempt to deal with the workload had hurt the company.

In retrospect, it was clear that the vaunted culture at the highest management levels had assaulted Andesa's ethical environment. We had fallen into the age-old trap of allowing the end to justify the means. We knew better than to take on a challenging venture without rock-solid support to back it up. We should have recognized in 2004 our weakness and made the hard choice to build a stronger, more capable senior management team before attempting any new ventures. As painful as it is to say, we allowed the allure of transient opportunities to justify the decision to move ahead without proper preparation.

What had gone wrong? Did our culture fail us? No, we failed our culture. In particular, we had failed to be willing to pay the short-term price, as we had when we hired Bill Smith, in order to be certain that the CEO hires were fully compatible with our culture.

As it turns out, our culture saved us from a series of management failures at the board and senior management levels. The staff pitched in and worked exceedingly hard to repair the damage. The shareholders accepted the need to dispense with financial distributions, and eventually we lowered our stock price by thirty-five percent. It was difficult, and no one was happy with the painful consequences of our mistakes, but we all hung together. Andesa would not be abandoned. The firm and its environment meant too much to its people for us to give up on it.

The situation was not altogether bleak. As we have seen before in the history of Andesa, adversity can be a form of inspiration, something that brings out the best in an individual, or in this case two individuals. Ron Scheese (Andesa's CFO) and Rick Kendall (Andesa's CTO) had both been with Andesa for less than a year when we terminated our CEO, yet they rose to the challenge of saving the company. In addition to doing their jobs, they stepped up and volunteered to help me with clients as we worked through the change.

In January, Rick met me at the Newark International Airport, and we visited two clients. The first meeting was with the firm that became a client in 2004. In spite of enormous expenditures of money and key staff, Andesa had failed to serve the client well. We had a candid discussion with the client and left the meeting with a clear agreement of the problems on both sides and a plan of action. As of today, we have reestablished a good relationship with this client in great part due to Rick and Ron's heroic efforts on the part of Andesa.

We met with another client and worked through a number of issues that had been festering for some time. That client is now one of our strongest advocates. Rick prepared for both meetings by doing extensive background work. As I shifted to the task of finding the next CEO, Rick and Ron continued to work with our client base. They were also the on-site de facto co-CEOs. Their efforts were readily accepted and appreciated by the staff. Because they were so obviously working hard for the good of the firm, no one questioned their authority to assume this role with only a few months' experience with Andesa.

Six or so months later, I once again visited with Keith Hurst. This time he appeared ebullient. He was relaxed and clearly looking forward to our discussion. I smiled at the satisfaction on his face and asked him how things were going.

"John, we're back on the right track. I've got some good help, and I'm enjoying my work again." Before I left, he told me that he and his wife had just bought a new home, a move they had been postponing because of the issues at Andesa. He said he couldn't even imagine leaving the company now.

From December 2006 through April 2007, I worked closely with Jerry Weiss in the search for a new CEO. The process this time was active and exceedingly thorough. Jerry knew our culture well. He conveyed its nuances to candidates and carefully measured their value systems to determine their fit with our culture. Jerry projected enthusiasm and excitement about Andesa that inspired them to investigate the company further. At Jerry's urging we also significantly increased the salary level for the position. In May 2007 we hired Frank Memmo, who relocated from Kansas to take over the reins of Andesa. In August of 2009, we added Rich Yeni as the Vice President for Business Development. It had taken fifteen years, but we finally succeeded with the transition from an entrepreneurial firm to a managed firm. I cannot imagine the possibility of success, given what we had to overcome, without our environment and the people that it had attracted.

In January 2011, Frank Memmo resigned and was replaced as CEO by Ron Scheese.

*Chapter Nine*

## Concluding Remarks

Today, we at Andesa better understand that management must begin with values. We have learned that, regardless of the cost, the senior management of a firm must keep a vigilant eye on their moral compass. Those values are what, ultimately, will keep the firm on course. While ethical behavior should be expected from every employee of a firm, it is most crucial that it be modeled from above. Managers are in a unique position to convey the culture to new employees and reiterate it on a daily basis. At Andesa, a strong management team is now in place, and those managers are committed to an employee-centric environment. Once again, we are a strong and plucky company, with the added benefit that we are finally in a position to grow without debilitating disruption. The staff is no longer overly concerned about change, growth, or the operational absence of the firm's founder. Andesa's leaders know that it is their job to protect employees from the pressures of unethical business behavior. It is their job to ensure that every individual involved with Andesa understands that the company holds them and their ethics in high regard.

From the very beginning, we at Andesa have understood that high ethical standards are critical to the creation of a great firm. While we underestimated the need for vigilance in holding Andesa to the values that made us successful in the first place, especially in a growth environment, core values have ultimately influenced our responses to the slew of difficult situations we have faced. Unlike my father, whose strength of character was enough to guide him, we have needed, at times, the added strength of community to remind us of the way. And while these times were hard on Andesa, I do not apologize for them; times like these are the reason an ethical environment is essential to the health of any organization. Instead, I celebrate the fact that Andesa has the soul to redirect itself when needed.

I can close my eyes and see my father say in his clear, quiet voice, "Tell a man the truth and you don't have to remember what you told him." But ethics were much more than a convenience to him, and so they are to Andesa. Truth-telling eliminates a lot of baggage and frees people to focus on more constructive activity, but it is merely the tip of the ethical iceberg. As an example of values in the workplace, I present the following ways in which values have shaped Andesa and positively affected our employees, clients, and shareholders.

**Employees**

Providing an environment in which employees can blossom and flourish is the honest expression of Andesa's mission statement. Whereas Dad and I never really took the opportunity to discuss values, his actions spoke volumes. I will never forget the belligerence with which he protected the welfare of army soldiers in Germany. I believe that his words—"I'll be damned if I'll do that!"—were the seeds that eventually grew into my own concern for employees. Over the years, Andesa's environment has been a haven for good, honest individuals. People who dread a cutthroat business culture find respite in the ethical norms promoted by the firm. Rick Kendall, our Chief Technology Officer, succinctly referenced Andesa's efforts in this regard when he said, "For me, working at Andesa can be summed up in two sentences. Andesa is a place where I believe I can make a difference every day. It's the culture that has created this environment."

Our employees believe they are valued, respected, and treated as equals no matter their role. And they are. They typically say they have never experienced a work environment that equals Andesa's. The employee comes first. This is the foundation upon which Andesa was built.

Staff turnover is very low. When employees do leave it is because a spouse is transferred to another area, an exceptional opportunity presents itself, or there is a rare mismatch between the employee and the company.

New employees with prior work experience frequently comment that they never imagined that such a healthy work environment existed, that the culture at Andesa is even better than they expected. In today's disloyal work culture (both on the part of the employer and the employee), having employees with the tenure that Andesa enjoys speaks volumes for the quality of life within the organization.

An ethical environment, however, is a two-way street. Just as employees thrive in the honesty of Andesa's culture, the firm likewise benefits from the honesty of its staff. Rather than excuse mediocre performance, our people apply themselves with diligence, passion, and genuine care for Andesa's well-being. And they do this not because they are pushed to do so but because the environment proudly celebrates their honest efforts. Because of the good work of our employees, everyone involved with the firm is better off.

Our clients provide us with an important external measure of our employees. It is especially significant that year after year clients assign the highest rating of our firm to our staff's competence and attitude. Year after year, via surveys, annual review questionnaires, and unsolicited feedback, clients comment on the honesty, professionalism, character, kindness, and responsiveness of Andesa employees.

We honor the staff's exceptional efforts to the best of our ability. In addition to salary, we routinely acknowledge Andesa's unsung heroes by name and by their contribution or achievement.

**Clients**

Annual client surveys, conducted by an independent firm, confirm that we are true to our commitment of providing excellent services.

We are honest with our clients. A powerful example of this is written into our operating procedures and dictates how we charge for our services. In an overall market environment where charging for identical services can vary widely, we charge strictly in accordance with the effort required to provide a specific service. The following examples illustrate this approach.

- We are very careful with our pricing schedules. For example, we increase our rates from time to time to reflect quality improvements, but these rates apply only to firms who become clients after the change. If we make prospective pricing changes which would be beneficial to existing clients, we change their pricing accordingly. We never provide a new client with a pricing schedule better than those for existing clients. And lastly, we tailor schedules to meet unique situations, but we never use these schedules as a ruse for preferential pricing.

- We do a lot of development work on behalf of clients. From time to time we find ourselves undertaking the same or highly similar project for two clients. Even if we have already quoted a price for the first client, the advent of a similar request will lead us to revise downward the first client's quote and charge the second client a reduced amount. We do this because we believe it to be the right thing to do. Our clients, however, are not typically accustomed to such treatment. They are most appreciative.

While we have occasionally miscalculated in this respect, we decline to take on new clients if we perceive that they operate from a set of values at odds with our own *or* if their relationship with us will be detrimental to our current clients. We have, indeed, ended partnerships, loss of profits notwithstanding, when the actions of those partners threatened to cast a shadow on our hard-earned, solid reputation for doing honest business.

We enjoy strong relationships with our clients' staffs. When we visit with clients, we are greeted with genuine affection, not formal handshakes. People who come to Andesa for solutions understand that to us they are not simply a means to an end (making money) but partners we are genuinely interested in working with to achieve their goals as well as our own.

Andesa has never lost a client due to dissatisfaction with our service. Even when we have failed them miserably in the short-term, our ability to connect on a personal level with our partners and our brutal honesty have allowed us to work through problems to ultimately give our clients the service they desire. This dogged determination to fulfill our obligations has garnered us long-standing and loyal clients.

## Shareholders

We have a small group of carefully screened shareholders with whom we enjoy an honest, two-way relationship. Our shareholders wholeheartedly support our value system because we stand for honesty, hard work, loyalty, and commitment. Even when these values don't directly translate into profits, they always reflect the good names of our investors.

The Andesa shareholder's primary relationship with the firm is a financial one, motivated in part by the expectation of financial returns. Each shareholder knows, however, that insistence on short-term financial results is not an honest expectation. There is no entitlement to a specific return; the shareholder's role is both to bear the financial brunt of hard times and to reap the rewards of growth and prosperity in good times.

As a group, Andesa's shareholders have sacrificed short-term returns on their investment time after time in order to make sure the company was positioned to remain viable and grow, and to make sure employees are well compensated today and into the future.

Over the years, our shareholders have been rewarded handsomely, if somewhat erratically. After several years of sub-standard financial returns, they once again look upon their investment in Andesa as one of the most valued of their financial assets.

This book was written for two reasons. First, I wanted to aid in the preservation of Andesa's culture by documenting how it came into existence. Second, I wanted to share with the business community a business culture worthy of emulation.

Andesa is a living example that a firm can indeed be both ethical and financially successful. In fact, I propose that in order to remain viable in the long run, a firm must be ethical. It must have a soul, and it must be willing to pay the price to keep its soul. If a firm is to benefit its clients and shareholders, it must first live up to its obligations to its employees. The employees, in turn, will take care of the clients and shareholders. That, ultimately, is the purpose of the firm, and that is the way ethics work.

Andesa stands as an important demonstration that a firm built on ethical principles with a focus on the welfare of its employees can be successful by all measures. It is important to note that ethics are not a foolproof recipe for success in the marketplace. Having a soul means a firm will try to do the right thing, but it is not a guarantee that it will reap financial rewards. One must look no further than Andesa to see the difficulties a firm can face in spite of good intentions. However, I believe that without an ethical environment to guide its people through the myriad pitfalls of the business world, a firm is destined to fail. In the long run, a firm must have a moral compass. Just as the human soul arms us to lead a significant and joyful life, the soul of a firm is what guides it toward fulfillment of its obligation to society.

**Final Statement**

As with leading a good life, building a firm with a soul is not easy. A firm's leaders must diligently adhere to and maintain every aspect of an ethical environment.

- The purpose of the firm must be carefully articulated. While the firm performs many functions, the purpose of the firm is to provide an ethical environment in which employees can fully develop and apply their business skills in order to benefit the employee, the client, and the shareholder. What it does after that is the product of its employees.

- Values must guide the actions of the firm. Without core values, the effort to maintain the environment will be simply too great.

- Management personnel must themselves be ethical and fully embrace the purpose of the firm. Indeed, unless managers are energized by their efforts to build and maintain the ethical environment, they likely will fail. Their responsibility is so pervasive that I shudder at the thought of their burden if their work is not a labor of love.

- The firm's people must be selected carefully. Responsible, industrious, and honest individuals will thrive in a firm with soul. Others likely will suffer and negatively affect others.

- The hiring process must empower potential employees to actively participate in the interview. By providing information in advance about the environment, the firm can ensure that both parties are prepared to work effectively toward determining a good fit. It is unreasonable to expect success if only the employer actively participates.

- The accomplishments of the environment must be celebrated. Celebration helps to maintain the bond.

Management is, at times, a beastly job. It can be heart wrenching, exhausting, and thankless. But, at the same time, I know of no activity as satisfying as that of contributing to an environment within which people blossom. As Adlai Stevenson once said about patriotism, "[it] is not a short and frenzied outburst of emotion, but the tranquil and steady dedication of a lifetime." So it is with the building of a business. I have a framed copy of Stevenson's quote in my office as a constant reminder to battle the tyranny of the urgent. Creating a firm with soul is the work of a lifetime. It is also the chance of a lifetime.

I wish for you the rewards of being part of an employee-centric firm; a firm with a soul.

## *Appendix A*

## ANDESA TIMELINE

1978 John Walker joins Covert and Associates (CTA)

1980 Insurance unit of CTA created

Insurance unit implements an insurance benefits record-keeping system

1981 Linda Ellison (LE) joins CTA

CTA becomes The Andesa Corporation (TAC)

1982 LE joins John in the insurance unit

TAC is restructured. The Andesa Companies is formed, with TAC as a subsidiary

1983 Insurance unit implements second new system

Signal Companies taken on as first client using second new system

1985 The Andesa Companies' board vote of confidence in insurance unit

Unit has enough success to assure financial viability for The Andesa Companies

| | |
|---|---|
| 1986 | Kim Bohling joins the unit as financial analyst |
| 1987 | Bill Smith joins unit as computer specialist |
| | Insurance brokerage activities transferred to Mac Briggs |
| 1989 | Unit becomes independent company – Andesa, TPA |
| 1990 | John becomes CEO of Clark Bardes, Dallas, TX |
| 1993 | John returns to Andesa full-time |
| 1999 | Chuck Clement joins Andesa as COO |
| 2003 | Andesa and ADASTAR merge |
| 2004 | Andesa, TPA, becomes Andesa Services |
| | Heather Horvath joins company as Director of Human Resources |
| 2006 | Chuck Clement promoted to CEO |
| | Ron Scheese joins Andesa as CFO |
| | Rick Kendall joins Andesa as CTO |
| | John reassumes CEO position |
| 2007 | Frank Memmo joins Andesa as CEO and President |
| 2009 | Ron Scheese assumes additional responsibility of CAO |
| | Rich Yeni Joins Andesa as VP Business Development |
| 2011 | Frank Memmo leaves Andesa |
| | Ron Scheese becomes CEO and President |
| | Mark Wilkin joins Andesa as CFO |

*Appendix B*

# The Evolution of Andesa's Management Team

### Andesa Management Team January, 1989

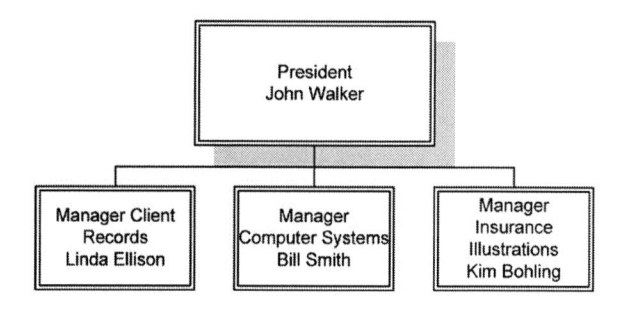

- **President** — John Walker
  - Manager Client Records — Linda Ellison
  - Manager Computer Systems — Bill Smith
  - Manager Insurance Illustrations — Kim Bohling

### Andesa Management Team May, 1999

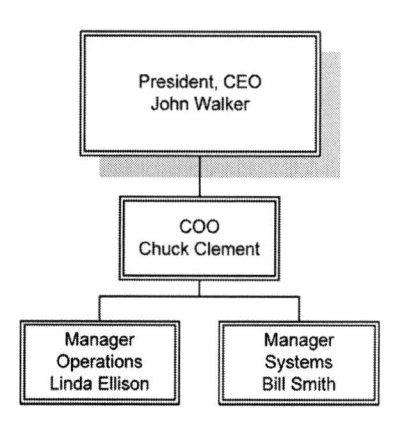

- **President, CEO** — John Walker
  - **COO** — Chuck Clement
    - Manager Operations — Linda Ellison
    - Manager Systems — Bill Smith

## Andesa Management Team July, 2003

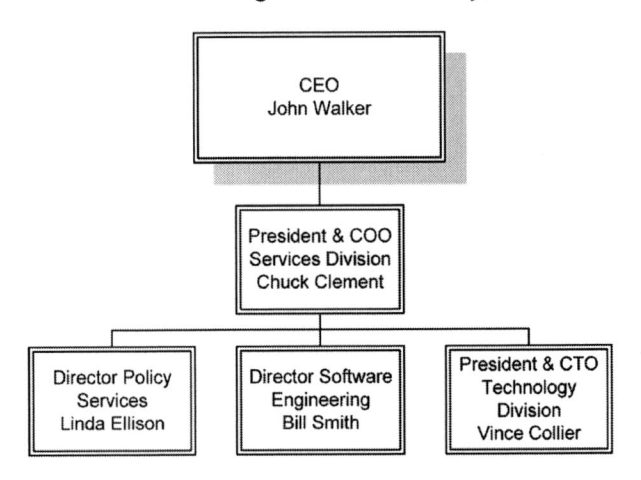

- CEO: John Walker
  - President & COO Services Division: Chuck Clement
    - Director Policy Services: Linda Ellison
    - Director Software Engineering: Bill Smith
    - President & CTO Technology Division: Vince Collier

## Andesa Management Team May, 2007

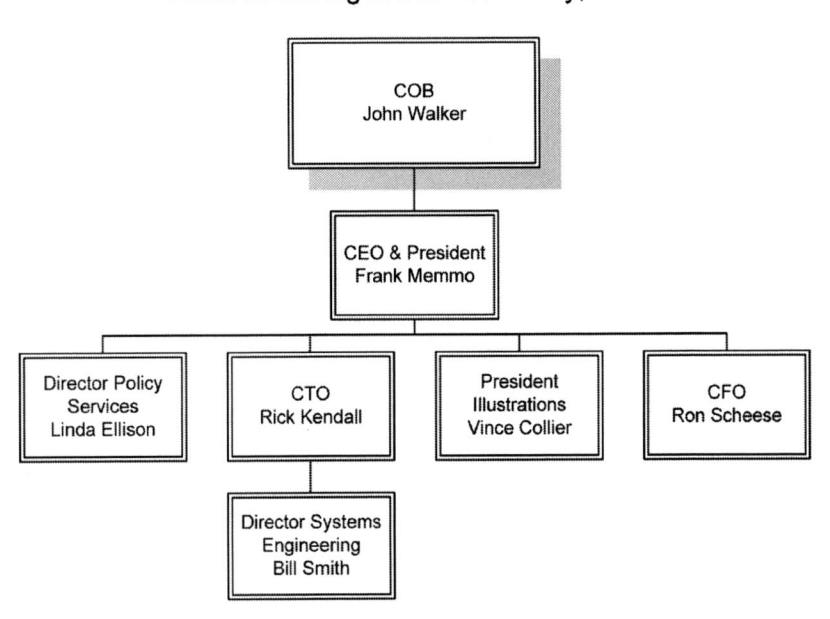

- COB: John Walker
  - CEO & President: Frank Memmo
    - Director Policy Services: Linda Ellison
    - CTO: Rick Kendall
      - Director Systems Engineering: Bill Smith
    - President Illustrations: Vince Collier
    - CFO: Ron Scheese